CAREERS in

ADVERTISING

VGM Professional Careers Series

ADVERTISING

S. WILLIAM PATTIS

THIRD EDITION

VGM Career Books

Chicago   New York   San Francisco   Lisbon   London   Madrid   Mexico City
Milan   New Delhi   San Juan   Seoul   Singapore   Sydney   Toronto

Library of Congress Cataloging-in-Publication Data

Pattis, S. William.
     Careers in advertising / S. William Pattis.—3rd ed.
        p.   cm.—(VGM professional careers series)
     ISBN 0-07-143049-0 (alk. paper)
     1. Advertising—Vocational guidance.   I. Title.   II. Series.

  HF5827.P378   2004
  659.1'023'73—dc22   2003025809

1 2 3 4 5 6 7 8 9 0 DOC/DOC 3 2 1 0 9 8 7 6 5 4

ISBN 0-07-143049-0

Interior design by Robert S. Tinnon

This book is printed on acid-free paper.

CONTENTS

Foreword   ix

Acknowledgments   xi

CHAPTER 1
The Evolution of Advertising   1
Advertising: A History • Advertising's Influence on the
Economy • Ethics, Codes, and Self-Imposed Regulations •
Advertising for the Public Good • Employment Opportunities
Today in the Advertising Profession

CHAPTER 2
Your Career in Creative Services   21
The Creative Team • The Copywriter • The Art Director •
The Broadcast Producer • The Creative Director • The
Creative Process

CHAPTER 3
Account Services: Putting It All Together   37
The Diversity of an Account Executive • Jobs in Account Services

CHAPTER 4
Media Services: Finding the Right Audience   47
Functional Components of Media Services • Execution of an
Effective Ad Campaign • Job Opportunities in Media Services

CHAPTER 5

Research: Defining the Consumer   57

Methods and Resources • The Skills of a Successful Researcher •
Job Opportunities in Research

CHAPTER 6

Opportunities in Traffic and Print Production   63

Traffic • Print Production • Job Opportunities in Traffic and
Print Production

CHAPTER 7

Agency Management and Administration   69

Agency Chief Executives • Financial Management •
Legal Services • Human Resources • Office Management •
Support Services

CHAPTER 8

**The Corporate Side:
Advertising and Brand Management   75**

Corporation vs. Agency • Corporate Advertising Departments •
Brand Management • Retail

CHAPTER 9

Working for a Media Company   81

Selling Space in Print Media • Job Opportunities in Print Media
Sales • Selling Space in Broadcast Media • Job Opportunities in
Broadcast Media Sales • The Qualities of a Good Media Sales
Representative • Other Opportunities

CHAPTER 10

**Public Relations, Publicity,
Sales Promotion, and Direct Mail   91**

Public Relations • Publicity • Sales Promotion • Direct Mail

CHAPTER 11

Interactive Advertising   97

Evolution of the World Wide Web and Web-Based Advertising •
Job Opportunities in Interactive Advertising

CHAPTER 12
Getting a Job and Moving Ahead   103
Career Information • Education and Training • Finding a Job • Where the Jobs Are • Getting Started • Résumés • Portfolios • Interviews • Making Your Decision • On-the-Job Training • Promotion and Advancement • Freelancing or Starting Your Own Agency • Opportunities in Smaller Agencies • Salaries • Wrap-Up • Organizations for Specific Groups

APPENDIX A
Recommended Reading, Websites, Directories, and Periodicals   131

APPENDIX B
College Advertising Programs   135

APPENDIX C
National Groups and Associations   143

FOREWORD

Hollywood stars, sports celebrities, supermodels—there's plenty of reasons to be attracted to the glamorous field of advertising. Every time we turn on the radio or television, sign on to the Internet, or read a newspaper or magazine, we experience the product of the world's most creative industry. The spokespeople are gorgeous, the special effects are dazzling, and the music and video techniques are the ultimate in "cool."

That's the public face of advertising, and it is so compelling that we sometimes forget that the business of advertising hides behind that fashionable mask. Advertising is a monster force in the global marketplace, compelling product sales, motivating consumers, promoting ideas, and generally supporting all forms of mass media. Tens of thousands of employees conceive, create, write, and produce the print ads, television spots, websites, and direct-mail solicitations and manage the media process that brings them into our homes.

According to *Advertising Age*, the advertising industry newspaper of record, U.S. advertisers spend more than $225 billion each year on advertising—more than many foreign countries spend on public services for their citizens. General Motors alone spends nearly $3.5 billion—just to sell automobiles!

Where there is that much wealth, there is also a wealth of opportunity, and this career guide to advertising provides a solid nuts-and-bolts introduction to the advertising industry—what makes it tick, who makes it work, and how to get started on the path to success.

If you are interested in a career in advertising, then you've got to know what's behind the glitz.

This guide explores the depth and breadth of the advertising industry and the broad range of career choices it harbors, including account services, agency management, brand management, creative services, media sales, media services, print and broadcast production, public relations, research, and traffic.

Careers in Advertising also provides a snapshot of advertising agency operations, the most significant source of industry opportunities, and suggests training and education for entry-level job seekers. It's a great place to get started in your career planning.

If you're smart, creative, and willing to work hard, there's probably a job for you in the world of advertising—and you may even get to hang out with celebrities!

LEN STRAZEWSKI
Journalism Department
Columbia College Chicago

ACKNOWLEDGMENTS

For whatever reason you picked up this book, you obviously have an interest in advertising. Good for you! If that interest is to seek a career, then read on, because you have chosen a dynamic profession that demands creativity, hard work, unpredictable hours, and the ability to ride the crest of success or handle the frustration of defeat. You will find it all in advertising, and if you happen to be really good, you'll enjoy the work even more and probably make a pile of money.

I have spent over fifty years in the fast-paced world of advertising and publishing, and my family has had to share it all. Therefore, I would like to dedicate this book to my one and only wife of fifty-three years, Bette, and my adult children and their spouses, Mark and Anne-Françoise Pattis of Highland Park, Illinois, and Robin and Roger Himovitz of Montecito, California. Also, a special mention goes to my five wonderful grandchildren—Rachael, Benjamin, Jacob, and Eli Himovitz and Madeleine Annette Pattis—with the hope that this book will give them a little more by which to remember "Popi" in the years to come.

Finally, I owe a very special thanks to Len Strazewski, former editor at *Advertising Age* and now on the journalism faculty at Columbia College Chicago, for his splendid research and help in assembling this book.

1

THE EVOLUTION OF ADVERTISING

You already know a lot about advertising. It's all around you, in every medium you experience every day—signing, shouting, flashing messages about products, services, events, activities—anything that can be bought, sold, or experienced for a price.

Advertising permeates nearly every facet of modern society. You would be hard pressed to find anyone or any modern culture unaffected by advertising. The process is designed to be inclusive—to reach out to everyone. For example, businesses advertise to make the consumer aware of the products or services they provide and hope that this awareness results in increased sales or improved public acceptance. In some instances, advertisers seek to promote a particular idea or cause through their advertising. Besides informing the public of the goods and services available in the marketplace, advertising also helps create a public image for the advertiser. A company's ads can say a lot about that company's personality, style, and credibility or lack thereof. Because advertising serves as the advertiser's link to the buying public, public perception becomes crucial to a company's ultimate success.

Businesses employ a variety of electronic and traditional media to reach the public, and the mix of media in any advertising campaign continues to evolve as technology evolves. Television and radio are the broadcast mainstays. Newspapers, magazines, direct mail, billboards, posters, catalogs, and brochures are the traditional cornerstones of many advertising programs. Since the early 1990s, the Internet has joined the older media as an advertising tool, and its World Wide Web has become a fast-growing marketing and publishing vehicle, taking advantage of the global reach and interactive nature of the network technology.

Most of these media depend on advertising for a major portion of their revenues. The majority of radio and television networks and independent stations are funded by advertising revenue, and the success of radio and television programming is measured in part by its ability to generate advertising revenue. Most newspapers and magazines depend on advertising to pay their publication costs and to generate a profit.

Some media are designed exclusively for advertising. Without advertising, there would be little need for billboards, posters, and most catalogs.

Advertising's importance to the communications industry is immeasurable. In fact, most forms of media that the public takes for granted would be extremely expensive to the reader or viewer or would simply be out of business without the revenues produced by advertising. Advertising's importance in today's world should not be minimized; advertising dollars truly keep American media thriving.

The word *advertising* stems from the French verb *advertir*, meaning "to warn or call attention to." The American Marketing Association in Chicago (marketingpower.com) offers this definition: "the paid, nonpersonal presentation of goods, services, and ideas by an identified sponsor."

The distinguishing word in this definition is *paid*. Media can support product sales or image in many ways, but advertisers usually have to pay for the promotion of their products, services, or ideas and produce the content that conveys their message. In return, they control the message they want to communicate.

Publicity or positive mentions in the otherwise unrelated content of publications or broadcast programs can be thought of as free advertising. Publicity spreads the word about a product or service and is purely informational or simply entertaining for the audience, but it is a voluntary occurrence on the part of the medium. Because the advertiser has not paid for specific time or space to promote the product or service, the advertiser does not have the same level of control. This measure of control is why "paid" is a key part of the definition of advertising.

The American Marketing Association's definition of advertising also lends a deeper understanding of the field. The term *nonpersonal* implies that the message is intended to reach a large group of people rather than a specific person. Advertising is not personal, one-to-one selling, but is accomplished through the mass media. Internet advertising, however, poses some exceptions. Since websites are cheap and easy to produce, they can be designed to attract a very narrow audience and allow individuals to make purchase decisions at the same time they view online advertising. E-mail advertising—online communication to individuals who have special interests—is a high-tech offshoot of direct marketing and can target individuals or small groups of similar individuals.

The phrase "goods, services, and ideas" shows that advertising covers a wide range of consumer needs. Advertising promotes more than products or goods, but also services, such as those offered by dry cleaners, banks, restaurants, and repair shops. Besides services, there is a growing trend to promote ideas through advertising. One look at the amount of paid political advertising during an election campaign reveals the importance of advertising in communicating ideas. The campaigner uses advertising to influence voters to accept his or her political ideas and support his or her quest for political office. Television advertising is the fastest way to reach the greatest number of voters and the most popular medium for political advertisers and has, unfortunately, led to an unprecedented amount of negative advertising and personal attacks by candidates. With these developments, it is clear that advertising is far more complex than simply selling a can of soup.

Continuing the definition, an "identified sponsor" allows the viewer or reader of the advertisement to identify the producer of the product, the company offering the service, or the group promoting the idea. Advertising usually reveals the brand name of the product, enabling viewers or readers to identify the product with the producer. Obviously, it would be pointless to advertise without indicating the sponsor and brand name, though some modern advertising has become obscure on identification as it attempts to emphasize image development over sales.

Besides placing ads in the various forms of media, advertisers can also employ consumer promotions, trade promotions, and point-of-purchase advertising. Consumer promotions include coupons, special sales, contests, or any type of special offering that attempts to persuade the consumer to purchase a product or service. Trade promotions consist of special offers made to wholesalers and retailers such as "Buy 1,000 units and get 100 free" or "Order before this date and receive no bill until a later date." Exhibits and trade shows also fall under the umbrella of trade promotions.

Point-of-purchase advertising occurs at the location where the product is made available for sale or use. This type of advertising can include unique product displays, banners, posters, neon signs, and other eye-catching devices. Point-of-purchase advertising draws attention to the product right where the consumer is—in the supermarket, convenience store, or elsewhere. It often has a great effect because it can make a product stand out from the other products, and the consumer can purchase the product right then and there on impulse. The immediacy of point-of-purchase advertising makes it a powerful tool for the advertiser.

The advertising process is very much a chain of activity, beginning with the company that produces a product or service and ending with the consumer who makes a buying decision. Advertising provides a connection between someone offering something and someone who needs something. In the middle of this chain is the link that connects producers and consumers—the advertising agencies.

Advertising agencies play a crucial role in today's advertising business. These organizations are responsible for creating, producing, and placing ads for their clients' companies or institutions and developing the strategies that stimulate the recognition, image, and sales their clients desire. Advertising agencies may also provide assistance in other areas, such as sales and marketing, public relations, and market research. Agency size can range from a few people to thousands, but within each agency, large or small, one or more people handle the different functions needed to produce the ads and to see that they appear in the right place at the right time.

Many of the most dynamic and creative job opportunities in the advertising business are within advertising agencies, but after years of remarkable growth, the advertising industry has suffered a recent downturn and a shift toward corporate advertising. As a result, there are also many job opportunities in the advertising or "brand management" departments of corporations.

ADVERTISING: A HISTORY

Advertising, in one form or another, has been going on since ancient times. By reviewing the development of advertising through the ages, it's easy to see how advertising has grown to its present level of influence and importance. Even though early advertising was simple compared with today's standards, the basic reason for advertising was the same then as now—to communicate information about products, services, and ideas to groups of people.

Early craftspeople were among the world's first advertisers. To identify their work, they would place individual marks or trademarks on their goods. Similar to the brand names that we look for today while shopping for merchandise, these trademarks indicated to buyers which craftsperson created a particular object. As the reputation of a particular craftsperson increased, people would look for that trademark when buying goods. The trademark's usefulness in the world of commerce has a long history. Even today it protects manufacturers from those who would pass off inferior products under that manufacturer's name, and it protects consumers by ensuring that they can purchase the products they desire.

Signs used by tradespeople to state the nature of their business were found in the ruins of Babylon. Since few people could read, these signs showed pictures of the product or service for sale—a loaf of bread for a bakery, a boot for a shoemaker's shop. Excavations at Pompeii reveal a similar use of signs to indicate the type of shop and what they offered for sale. In ancient Egypt, items for sale and messages of interest were carved into stone tablets called stelae and placed on roads for the passersby to read. These tablets were the precursors to today's billboards.

The spoken word played a role in advertising long before the advent of radio and television. Men were paid to walk the streets in ancient Greece telling the citizens of news and public events. These men were known as town criers. In Egypt, town criers told of the arrival of new merchandise arriving on ships.

Movable printing, invented by the Chinese, made printed handbills possible. Handbills were the earliest printed advertisements and were often bound into books. A handbill would usually show the sign that hung over the door of a particular shop and include brief copy underneath in script. The invention of the printing press in 1450 helped handbills evolve into the first newspaper—and almost as soon as the presses were rolling, they were being used for advertising. By the middle of the seventeenth century, weekly newspapers began to appear in England, and soon the British became the world leader in advertising. Newspapers enticed businesses into advertising their products on a grander scale. The most frequent early newspaper advertisers were importers of products new to the British Isles. For example, when coffee first became available in England in 1652, it was announced in a newspaper ad.

The first documented appearance of competitive advertising, as opposed to the simple announcement of new products being made available to the public, occurred in the early eighteenth century. In 1710, patent medicine advertisements appeared that attempted to persuade readers of one product's superiority to another similar product. Though many of the claims made in these early ads may seem incredible and exaggerated to us today, this type of advertising is still extremely common.

The Crown's tax on both British newspapers and their advertisements severely curtailed the expansion of the advertising industry in England. In fact, this tax represented one of the grievances the American colonists held against the British government during the American Revolution. After the Revolution, the United States soon surpassed Britain to become the world leader in advertising.

With the invention of the steam engine and the advent of the Industrial Revolution in the mid-nineteenth century, advertising's influence expanded greatly. The Civil War created the need for mass production, and as the country grew, so did the need for factory-made goods. At the same time, manufacturers needed to spread the word about their products to an expanding consumer base and consequently turned to advertising to do the job. By communicating the availability of products to more people, sales increased, thus allowing manufacturers to produce more and consequently charge less for their products. In this way, advertising helped fuel the Industrial Revolution.

Transportation represented another important element in the rapidly expanding economy of the nineteenth century. Without an efficient and all-encompassing transportation system, goods cannot get to the markets where they are needed. In the United States, the railroad provided the system whereby these goods found their way around the country. By the 1890s, the entire country was connected by railroads, helping create a more unified market rather than a group of local and regional markets. Other technological innovations helped fuel the remarkable growth of the advertising industry in the late nineteenth century. These included the invention of the rotary press in 1849, the manufacturer of paper from wood pulp in 1866, the arrival of the linotype in 1884, and the invention of halftone engraving in 1893.

As the economy grew, so did the number of newspapers and magazines and thus the number of ads placed. In 1830, there were 1,200 U.S. newspapers; by 1860, there were about 3,000; the peak was reached in 1914 when there were 15,000 newspapers in circulation in this country. In 1850, there were approximately 700 magazines in the United States, and by 1880 this number had grown to 2,400; by 1900, it had doubled to 4,800. As the number of magazines and newspapers increased, advertising became more prevalent than ever before.

Before the mid-nineteenth century, merchants wrote and placed their own advertising in local magazines and newspapers. With the Industrial Revolution, many businesses were eager to expand their sales into broader markets. Soon, publishers of newspapers and magazines hired advertising agents to help them sell advertising to retailers and manufacturers. These agents acted as liaisons between the publisher and the advertiser, and the ads were usually prepared by the advertiser or the agent. These advertising agents functioned as the first advertising agencies. Often, agents were hired by the publishers, not the advertisers. Other so-called agents were simply brokers of space. They would negotiate to buy space in a newspaper or magazine at a low rate and then sell this space to an advertiser for a higher rate to make a profit. As a result of this practice, advertising agents often gained a bad reputation but still took their place in the chain of the advertising process.

N. W. Ayer, an advertising agency pioneer, helped change this negative perception of the advertising business by instituting a major shift in the focus of the entire advertising system in the late 1860s. Ayer believed that it would be better to represent the interests of the advertisers rather than those of the publishers. Thus, Ayer started the first advertising agency and based it on this concept. He hired writers and artists and persuaded advertisers that his company could create effective advertising that would result in increased sales for the advertiser. Ayer not only brought organization and order to the advertising business, but also gave it a much-needed boost of credibility.

By the beginning of the twentieth century, advertising agencies had taken on the role they fill today, a hundred years later, including the creation, organization, and execution of advertising campaigns for their clients. The twentieth century also brought a communications revolution that fueled unprecedented growth in the advertising industry. Radio and television brought the advertiser's message to millions of potential consumers instantly. No longer did advertisers have to rely on the printed word to get their message across. Even those who could not read could be reached through these new tools of mass communication. Guglielmo Marconi transmitted the first wireless message in 1895. By 1922, there were thirty radio stations licensed by the Federal Communications Commission (FCC). In 1926, NBC became the first broadcasting company to air the same program all over the country. In the 1930s and 1940s, the radio industry experienced great growth and became a formidable influence in people's lives. It was also during this period that the practice of using popular celebrities to endorse products first became common. Today, celebrity endorsements often play a vital role in the success of a product.

Commercial radio made it possible for national advertisers to reach large numbers of people and to expand their coverage of the market. In the early days of radio, many advertisers and their products sponsored entire shows, such as the *Texaco Star Theater* and the *Jell-O Program*, which garnered large, devoted audiences. By associating a product with a popular radio show, both the company's image and their sales benefited. Today, there are more than twelve thousand radio stations in the United States alone, and advertisers spend about to $18 billion a year on radio advertising, according to *Advertising Age*.

Television's arrival on the scene in the 1950s signaled the end of radio's dominance and the beginning of another boom in the advertising industry. The ability to reach millions of households with a visual image led to further growth for the advertising industry. In the 1950s, television sets were the fastest-selling appliances on the market, and advertising dollars began to shift from radio and print media to television. Advertisers who had been using only words and still pictures to sell their products now could combine sight, sound, and motion in their message. By 1955, advertisers were spending more than $1 billion a year on television advertising.

In 2001, advertisers spent nearly $39 billion on broadcast television. To illustrate the power of TV advertising, a thirty-second commercial or "spot" on prime-time TV may be seen in more than 100 million U.S. households at the same time. As advertisers have discovered, the effect that television advertising has on sales is staggering.

Beginning in the 1970s, cable television added another lucrative and creative dimension to television advertising. Like broadcast television, cable TV airs conventional spots, but offers advertisers additional opportunity to target audiences committed to specific content or activities. Food Network viewers, for example, have a more focused interest in food products and preparation. In 2001, advertisers spent more than $15 billion on cable television advertising.

Some cable networks, such as QVC and The Shop at Home Network, allow viewers to actually buy the products they see on television from the comfort of their own home. Others offer half-hour or hour-long paid commercials called "infomercials."

Beginning in the mid-1990s, Internet advertising took its place in the advertising media mix. Viewed by home and office computer users using graphic readers called browsers, Internet advertising runs the gamut from "banner" ads placed above or below Web page content to more interactive catalogs and ordering systems that present an advertising message and allow viewers to place orders online. In 2001, advertisers spent more than $5 billion in Internet advertising.

ADVERTISING'S INFLUENCE ON THE ECONOMY

In the economic doldrums of the early twenty-first century, the question of advertising's effect on the economy is a cause for great debate in the advertising industry. Some argue that advertising makes a great contribution to the economy, while others downplay advertising's role in this area. From the sheer volume of dollars spent on advertising every year and the way advertising facilitates the sale of products and services, there is no denying advertising's influence on the U.S. economy. Measuring that influence is another matter.

Advertising plays an important role in the distribution of goods and services, and the demand created by advertising helps the economy to expand. The cost of advertising is included in the cost of the product or service, but those who advertise know that advertising translates into sales and that costs can be reduced through the increased production caused by increased demand. Advertising can mean the difference between success and failure for the advertiser. As much as one-third of the total sales, manufacturing, and marketing expense of low-cost, frequently purchased products is spent on advertising. This highlights the importance that marketers attach to advertising.

Advertising's economic influence varies widely from product to product. Advertising contributes most to the sales of products such as cosmetics, medicines, cereals, candy bars, and other packaged goods. Advertising plays a lesser role in the sales of products such as industrial equipment or boats, for example. Goods and services sold by direct mail depend exclusively on advertising because it is the only way for buyers to learn how and where to purchase these goods and services.

If advertising influences the economy, it is also clear that the economy influences advertising. The recessions of 1980–81 and 1990–92 had a great impact on the advertising industry. These economic downturns led to decreases in billings as well as layoffs within the industry, proving that the same industry that helps to fuel the economy suffers when the economy takes a turn for the worse. In the recession of 2001–03, advertising again reflected the downturn. Total advertising spending dropped 6.5 percent to $231.4 billion from 2001 to 2002, according to *Advertising Age*.

ETHICS, CODES, AND SELF-IMPOSED REGULATIONS

The amount of misleading or false advertising has decreased over the years owing to the influence of government intervention through various laws, codes, regulations, and principles. In the United States, the Federal Trade Commission (FTC) monitors advertising to decide whether it is false or misleading. The FTC may require advertisers to provide proof of their claims or may order advertisers to remove ads that are considered questionable. Specific types of advertising are regulated by other government agencies.

Although these agencies are concerned with the public welfare and believe that they know what is "right," advertisers often have their own concept of what is "right" and often disagree with the judgments of these agencies. Until a reasonable consensus can be reached, advertisers and government agencies will continue to be at odds on certain issues.

The advertising industry's concern with maintaining respectability and truth in advertising has resulted in several voluntary associations that operate under self-imposed regulations designed to discourage and penalize improper or unethical practices. These organizations include the American Association of Advertising Agencies (AAAA), the Association of National Advertisers (ANA), the National Association of Broadcasters (NAB), which

regulate what airs on television and radio, along with the Magazine Publishers Association (MPA) and the American Association of Business Publishers (AABP), which monitor the advertising content of magazines and
newspapers. Two organizations publish formal codes of ethics (see below
and pages 12 and 13).

The National Advertising Division (NAD) of the Council of Better
Business Bureaus, formed by agencies and advertisers, reviews complaints

THE ADVERTISING CODE OF AMERICAN BUSINESS*

Truth
Advertising shall tell the truth, and shall reveal significant facts, the concealment of
which would mislead the public.

Substantiation
Advertising claims shall be substantiated by evidence in possession of the advertiser
and advertising agency, prior to making such claims.

Comparisons
Advertising shall refrain from making false, misleading, or unsubstantiated statements
or claims about a competitor or his/her products or services.

Bait Advertising
Advertising shall not offer products or services for sale unless such offer constitutes
a bona fide effort to sell the advertising products or services and is not a device to
switch consumers to other goods or services, usually higher priced.

Guarantees and Warranties
Advertising of guarantees and warranties shall be explicit, with sufficient information
to apprise consumers of their principal terms and limitations or, when space or time
restrictions preclude such disclosures, the advertisement should clearly reveal where
the full text of the guarantee or warranty can be examined before purchase.

Price Claims
Advertising shall avoid price or savings claims which are false or misleading, or which
do not offer provable bargains or savings.

Unprovable Claims
Advertising shall avoid the use of exaggerated or unprovable claims.

Testimonials
Advertising containing testimonials shall be limited to those of competent witnesses
who are reflecting a real and honest opinion or experience.

*Adopted by the American Advertising Federation Board of Directors, March 2, 1984,
San Antonio, Texas.

STANDARDS OF PRACTICE OF THE
AMERICAN ASSOCIATION OF ADVERTISING AGENCIES

First adopted October 16, 1924
Most recently revised September 18, 1990

We hold that a responsibility of advertising agencies is to be a constructive force in business.

We hold that, to discharge this responsibility, advertising agencies must recognize an obligation, not only to their clients, but to the public, the media they employ, and to each other. As a business, the advertising agency must operate within the framework of the competition. It is recognized that keen and vigorous competition, honestly conducted, is necessary to the growth and the health of American business. However, unethical competitive practices in the advertising agency business lead to financial waste, dilution of service, diversion of manpower, loss of prestige, and tend to weaken public confidence both in advertisements and in the institution of advertising.

We hold that the advertising agency should compete on merit and not by attempts at discrediting or disparaging a competitor agency, or its work, directly or by inference, or by circulating harmful rumors about another agency, or by making unwarranted claims of particular skills in judging or prejudging advertising copy.

To these ends, the American Association of Advertising Agencies has adopted the following Creative Code as being in the best interests of the public, the advertisers, the media, and the agencies themselves. The AAAA believes the Code's provisions serve as a guide to the kind of agency conduct that experience has shown to be wise, foresighted, and constructive. In accepting membership, an agency agrees to follow it.

Creative Code

We, the members of the American Association of Advertising Agencies, in addition to supporting and obeying the laws and legal regulations pertaining to advertising, undertake to extend and broaden the application of high ethical standards. Specifically, we will not knowingly create advertising that contains:

- a. False or misleading statements or exaggerations, visual or verbal
- b. Testimonials that do not reflect the real opinion of the individual(s) involved
- c. Price claims that are misleading
- d. Claims insufficiently supported or that distort the true meaning or practicable application of statements made by professional or scientific authority
- e. Statements, suggestions, or pictures offensive to public decency or minority segments of the population

We recognize that there are areas that are subject to honestly different interpretations and judgment. Nevertheless, we agree not to recommend to an advertiser, and to discourage the use of, advertising that is in poor or questionable taste or that is deliberately irritating through aural or visual content or presentation.

Comparative advertising shall be governed by the same standards of truthfulness, claim substantiation, tastefulness, etc., as apply to other types of advertising.

These Standards of Practice of the American Association of Advertising Agencies come from the belief that sound and ethical practice is good business. Confidence and respect are indispensable to success in a business embracing the many intangibles of agency service and involving relationships so dependent upon good faith.

Clear and willful violation of these Standards of Practice may be referred to the Board of Directors of the American Association of Advertising Agencies for appropriate action, including possible annulment of membership as provided by Article IV, Section 5, of the Constitution and By-Laws.

about misleading or false advertising. The NAD goes so far as to investigate complaints and arrange settlements between parties. If no settlement can be reached, an appeal can be made to the National Advertising Review Board, a five-member body with representatives from advertising and the public sector. This board has the power to pull or change advertising that it considers questionable.

Despite the efforts of these regulatory groups, abuses and false advertising claims still occur, though less and less frequently. Public taste and social mores also pose problems for the advertising agencies. Advertising creators often challenge public standards as they strive to create distinctive, attention-getting advertisements for their clients.

ADVERTISING FOR THE PUBLIC GOOD

The Advertising Council represents one of the most important and influential organizations in the advertising industry. The Ad Council develops public service announcements (PSAs) and other forms of advertising dedicated to the improvement of society as a whole. It coordinates advertisers, advertising agencies, and media in its efforts to create effective public service messages and deliver those messages to the public. All creative time, effort, and media are contributed (no charge) for the general public welfare. About one-third of all PSAs are Ad Council campaigns.

Ad Council campaigns also include programs targeted to specific causes or groups, often focusing on reversing the effects of patterns of discrimination on minority groups.

The efforts of the Ad Council provide the advertising industry with a way to use its talents and resources to help people; over the last fifty years, the work of the Ad Council has had an extremely positive effect in this country. Beginning with the World War II slogan "Loose lips sink ships" through the well-known Smokey Bear's "Only you can prevent forest fires" and the United Negro College Fund's "A mind is a terrible thing to waste," the Ad Council has made its mark in the public's thoughts and been instrumental in changing behavior.

For example, 1992 marked the first year since the 1940s that automobile fatalities dropped below 40,000, an achievement for which the government gave considerable credit to the Ad Council's "Buckle up" and "Friends don't let friends drive drunk" campaigns, which began a few years prior. In later years, Ad Council campaigns contributed to the public understanding of heart disease and cholesterol, high blood pressure, and acquired immune deficiency syndrome (AIDS).

Here are some of the causes supported by the Advertising Council in 2003:

- ACT Against Violence
- After School Alliance
- AIDS awareness
- Americans for the Arts
- Big Brothers, Big Sisters
- Child abuse prevention
- Childhood asthma
- Colon cancer prevention and detection
- Community drug prevention
- Crime prevention (adults and kids)
- Domestic violence prevention
- Drunk driving prevention
- Family literacy
- Firewise
- Girls Go Tech

- Give Kids the World
- Homeland security
- Housing discrimination
- Learning disabilities
- Library of Congress
- The Martin Luther King Jr. Memorial
- National Trust for Historic Preservation
- Operation Graduation
- Partners for Public Education
- Racial cooperation
- Seat belt education
- Stroke Early Response
- United Negro College Fund
- Wildfire prevention

There are also many charities, educational institutions, and social service agencies that use advertising to inform people about public concerns or to solicit contributions. Besides possible projects with the Ad Council, almost every sizable agency as well as many advertisers and members of the media have one or two civic, charitable, or educational projects that they back at their own expense and through support from members of the media.

Advertising agencies are also employed by many government agencies to promote certain branches of the government. In 2001, the U.S. government was the twenty-fourth largest advertiser in the country, spending about $1 billion. The largest share of these dollars are spent on advertising for the military—the army, navy, air force, and marines. The U.S. Postal Service employs advertising as a means to increase public use of the postal services. Government advertising creates special circumstances for the advertising industry, since all dealings with the federal government are subject to a great many safeguards and regulations.

In standard commercial transactions involving an advertiser and an agency, oral agreements are all that are required to start things rolling, and large amounts of money are committed as a result of these understandings. But when doing business with the federal government, an advertising agency cannot undertake any new projects or bind the government to any financial obligation without first completing a great deal of paperwork to get legal authority for the plan. As a result of these restrictions, many advertising agencies employ specialists to deal with the administration and management of government contracts. This may be an area of special interest for some individuals seeking a career in the advertising industry.

EMPLOYMENT OPPORTUNITIES TODAY IN THE ADVERTISING PROFESSION

The twentieth-century expansion of the American economy had a dramatic effect on the advertising industry. The postwar boom of the 1950s and 1960s led to a great increase in the amount of money spent on advertising by American business. With more disposable income in the hands of Americans, businesses looked to advertising to spread the word about their products so they could cash in on the public's new spending habits. In 1950, American businesses spent $5.7 billion on advertising, practically twice as much as was spent in 1930. By the late 1980s, advertising expenditures had increased to more than $120 billion, and by 1990, advertising spending reached a high of $128 billion. The recession of the early 1990s, though, had a significant impact on an industry whose growth and opportunities seemed to be never-ending. Many who predicted continued growth for the advertising industry were disappointed when the industry suffered its first decrease in spending in thirty years, as total expenditures fell from $128 billion in 1990 to $126.4 billion in 1991. Although the industry rebounded in 1992 with spending increasing to $131 billion, the damage had been done. The recession, coupled with the "merger mania" of the 1980s, led to many lost jobs in the industry—7,600 in 1991 alone.

The first recession of the twenty-first century had a predictable impact. Advertising revenues that had boomed in the late 1990s fell 9.5 percent to $247.7 million in 2000 and continued to drop the following year, down 6.5 percent to $231.3 million. However, the following year, as advertisers regrouped, revenues began a slow climb upward, increasing 2.4 percent to $236.8 million.

What do these economic ups and downs mean for job seekers? Advertising jobs, like the industry itself, is extremely sensitive to the economy. By 2002, the advertising, broadcasting, and publishing industries lost nearly 150,000 jobs combined, including many senior positions. Mergers contributed to the loss of jobs as well-known advertising agencies formed new networks of shared ownership or were acquired by international conglomerates. For example, J. Walter Thompson Company and Young & Rubicam, two of the largest agencies in the 1990s, became members of the London-based WPP Group, along with several other agencies; the Interpublic Group of Companies expanded to include McCann-Erickson and Foote, Cone & Belding Worldwide; and Paris-owned Publicis Group acquired Leo Burnett and Saatchi & Saatchi.

Corporate advertising departments are extremely conservative in their hiring practices, keeping their brand management staffs lean even in the best of times. But advertising agencies expand and contract like an accordion, hiring furiously when they win new accounts and laying off staff when clients cut their budgets. However, despite the economic recovery beginning in 2003, jobs are not likely to increase substantially.

Entry-level positions, with their lower starting salaries, are somewhat insulated from this cycle, but the competition for entry-level positions can be fierce. The candidate who has prepared well for a career in advertising will fare the best in the quest for that coveted first job.

Often, the new agency employee starts out working as an assistant and learning the department operations from the inside out. For example, in the creative department, the production assistant learns print, TV and radio, and art production while helping the rest of the department with general office work. This position has great growth potential. Also in the creative department, the assistant copywriter helps the copywriters with editorial and proofreading work as well as general clerical duties. Strong language and writing skills are needed for this position. In the marketing department, the advertising assistant for sales can gain experience with sales representatives and clients while handling heavy phone work and typing. The media assistant assists the marketing department in the area of media operations with buying, planning, and scheduling. This work can also include preparing graphs and charts and taking part in client presentations. The enterprising employee will do his or her best in these entry-level jobs, no matter how menial some of the tasks may be. It is the employee who is eager to learn the business and help the agency in any way possible who can look forward to enjoying a long and rewarding career.

Corporate Advertising Departments

An area of great opportunity that is often overlooked by college graduates is the corporate advertising department. Here employees work for a single company and become involved with every aspect of advertising while also participating in the total marketing effort of their employer. Although most such corporate advertising departments use the services of an advertising agency, others have an in-house advertising agency complete with all the job opportunities that an outside agency offers. Young people generally gravitate toward the glamour of an advertising agency, but the corporate advertising department can be every bit as challenging and rewarding as the conventional advertising agency.

Marketing and advertising are highly regarded as key measures of success, so if you are responsible for a successful advertising campaign, you might be in position to earn a promotion to a senior executive position—even president! This is especially true in markets where advertising is the primary force in determining the success of the company—such as packaged goods, personal care products, fragrances, and travel. A business-minded graduate seeking a job in advertising would do well to consider opportunities for work at General Motors, or Procter and Gamble, the two largest U.S. advertisers, as well as McCann-Erickson Worldwide, BBDO Worldwide, J. Walter Thompson Company, or other large agency operations.

Primary Areas of Opportunity for Beginners

There are many areas in the advertising industry where beginners are likely to get their start. The following sampling of career areas corresponds with the areas covered in the chapters that follow. Keep in mind that these opportunities exist in both agency and corporate environments.

Creative Services

This is where the ads are created. The finished work includes print ads, radio and television commercials, direct mail, catalogs, packaging, and, in some cases, websites. Among the positions available in creative services in both agency and corporate settings are copywriter, art director, creative director, graphic artist, illustrator, photographer, TV producer, and digital or mechanical artist.

Account Management

Account executives in the agency setting represent the agency to the client and the client to the agency. They are responsible for coordinating the advertising campaign and making sure that the agency and the client are satisfied. In the corporate setting, the equivalent of account executives are generally the advertising managers or directors who have the same responsibilities except that they do not answer to the client, but to the company they work for. Positions in this area include management supervisor, account supervisor, account executive, account coordinator, and account assistant.

Media Services

Media planners evaluate and recommend where ads should be placed to reach the optimum audience and attain the best response. Media buyers negotiate and purchase space for ads in newspapers and magazines and time for commercials on radio and television. Other positions in media services include media director, media supervisor, broadcast media supervisor, and media estimator.

Research

Agency and nonagency researchers attempt to identify the audience that the client wants to reach. Researchers also test creative material to gauge its effectiveness in reaching and influencing the targeted audience.

Production and Traffic

Print production turns the copy and artwork into finished advertising, more and more frequently using computer-based digital graphics and editing tools. Broadcast production handles the making of a television or radio commercial from casting to the final edit. The traffic department schedules and keeps track of all production and creative work and makes sure that all ads are finished on schedule and delivered to the media on time.

Agency Management and Administration

These are the people who run the agency. Leadership positions in agencies include president, chief executive officer (CEO), partner, chief financial officer (CFO), and chief creative officer. The financial administrators oversee client fees and billings, talent payments, production costs, and all matters relating to salaries, expenses, and benefits while also making sure the agency prospers. Chief creative officers, a relatively new position, oversee the overall quality and creativity of the agency work.

Media Sales

A career in media sales involves the sale of advertising in media to advertisers and their agencies. Sales positions can be found in all types of media—magazines, newspapers, television, radio, and outdoor advertising firms. An often overlooked option for those seeking careers in advertising, media sales provides an excellent overview of the entire business owing to the many contacts one makes as a media sales representative.

Other areas of opportunity include public relations, direct mail, sales promotion, and marketing, all of which are discussed in Chapter 10.

2

YOUR CAREER IN CREATIVE SERVICES

The creative departments perform the most visible and probably the most challenging and demanding work in the advertising business. Success in creative work can be extremely rewarding both in income and in personal satisfaction. To see your own work in a magazine or on television and to know that your ideas contributed to the success of your client's product or service is a great source of personal pride. It can also be a great source of compensation, as top creative employees are often among the highest paid in an advertising agency.

Creative services attract young people. Agencies are always looking for fresh, new perceptions and ideas, and they are often found among young employees in touch with the popular culture of music, entertainment, and fashion. Creative services is where ads are prepared and where the reputation and success of an advertising agency is made or lost. While all agency functions are important and contribute in one way or another to the success of the advertising campaign, the end product—the advertising itself—is what the client is most interested in, since the advertising is what the public reads or hears and either responds to or ignores.

People in creative services include copywriters, artists, photographers, commercial (or "spot") producers, and creative directors. Any one of these people can be the originator of a bright new campaign, a brilliant idea, or a new approach that convinces the public to buy the advertised product. People in creative services strive to be first-rate professionals in their specialty.

THE CREATIVE TEAM

In the creative department, teamwork is essential in developing a successful advertising campaign. At most agencies, a copywriter and an art director work in tandem as the cornerstones of the creative process used to create the ads for the client. When a TV commercial is required, the team may consist of a copywriter, an art director, and a spot producer—all working under the direction of the creative director. The size and makeup of the creative department vary, of course, from agency to agency and are influenced by the nature of the services the agency provides. Still, almost all ads created today are the result of collaboration by many talented people.

Ads were not always created by teams. Bill Bernbach, the legendary creative director of Doyle Dane Bernbach, a pioneering agency, and leader of the creative revolution in the industry in the 1960s, is generally considered the person who first introduced the team concept. By pairing copywriters and art directors, he did away with the old system of having the copywriter first write the ad and then hand it to the art director for layout and design. The division of labor in the creative department is not set in stone. Art directors may have ideas for copy, and copywriters will frequently come up with great visual ideas. The creative process is give-and-take, the bouncing of ideas off one another that often results in innovative and effective advertising.

Though the creative process is a team effort, individuals still maintain separate identities and responsibilities and will follow career paths that parallel their specific work. An individual will apply for a specific job and will be teamed up later, usually by the director of the creative team. No two agencies have the same structure, but most have positions of copywriter, art director, producer, and creative director.

THE COPYWRITER

The copywriter writes ads, creating text and contributing to the development of the broader advertising concept. He or she is responsible for the script for TV and radio commercials, for the headlines and text of print ads in newspapers and magazines, for the message that appears on billboards, and for the product copy we see in catalogs and on the sides of cereal boxes and other consumer packaging—essentially all of the written words associated with advertising. The copywriter may also write interactive or nonsequential text used in Internet advertising.

The copywriter is responsible for the slogans, catchphrases, and taglines that are often the basis for an entire advertising campaign. For example, "Don't leave home without it" for American Express and "Fly the friendly skies" for United Airlines are slogans that have been used successfully year after year. Often, a few words created by a copywriter can define a company's public image. When slogans are proved successful, they are often used in TV and print ads for many years.

Writing copy is not the same as writing articles, books, or poetry. Although all such writing is creative, advertising copy has a more definite role in that it must sell or enhance the public image of a product or service. Furthermore, it has to be written to satisfy a client. Every ad must stand on its own, yet each ad must be fully integrated into a campaign that is consistent with the marketing objectives of the client. The copywriter must also be aware of competitive products and must write copy that positions the client's product favorably.

The copywriter's job does not end when the ad is written. In a television commercial, for example, copywriter, art director, and producer must decide on such elements as format, music, and special effects.

A copywriter's job is not without frustration. When the initial idea is complete, the copywriter will usually seek approval from the creative director, who then will show it to the account executives who deal directly with the client. Changes may be required, or the whole concept may be scrapped, and the copywriter must remain flexible and willing to revise the work. Copywriters in agencies are often required to participate in the presentation of the proposed ads to the client. The client may have suggestions for changes that, most likely, will have to be implemented, like it or not.

Take warning, prospective copywriters! The final creative product is often unrecognizable when compared with the copywriter's original work.

Jobs in Copywriting

The entry-level position in copywriting is junior copywriter. Junior copywriters work on a variety of projects to learn the basics of their new career. Because so many young people seek jobs in copywriting, starting salaries are low. Individuals can move up from junior copywriter to copywriter and then to senior copywriter, gradually gaining increased responsibilities and pay. As copywriters progress up the ladder, the work becomes more challenging and they have the opportunity to become involved in the conceptual side of creative advertising. The larger advertising agencies generally employ a copy director who oversees a staff of copywriters, decides who will get which assignment, and supervises the day-to-day activity of the copywriting staff.

What It Takes to Be a Copywriter

To be successful as a copywriter, a person must develop certain skills and personal attributes. Copy must be clear and persuasive and aimed directly at the audience for which the ad has been created. Depending on the situation, the style may be formal, informal, or technical, but in all cases it must succeed in getting across the central message of the advertising campaign. When promoting products and services, the best copywriters create ads that contain one simple idea expressed clearly, memorably, forcefully, and persuasively. When asked to communicate more complex ideas, copywriters must be clear, logical, and precise. A good copywriter must have the ability to express both simple and complex ideas in a manner that will bring about a response from the targeted audience.

It also helps if the copywriter has an appreciation and understanding of good design and illustration and how they work in harmony and contribute to the effectiveness of a good ad. An understanding of all elements of an ad by everyone on the creative side helps the creative team to function as a unified and versatile unit. Copywriters should recognize that the design and visual portion of a print ad or TV commercial are as important as the copywriter's words—maybe more so. Furthermore, the copywriter may be required to tailor the text to fit the visual elements of the ad. It also helps if the copywriter has an understanding of the technical side of advertising production to work within the bounds of production realities. Great concepts that cannot be executed have no value in the pragmatic world of advertising creativity.

Copywriters must know what has worked well in the past and need to take advantage of proven techniques that are known to be successful. It is as important to be creative in knowing how to use or modify that which was proved successful as it is to create original concepts.

Copywriters also need a thorough understanding of the legal issues affecting claims that are made in promoting an advertised product or service. Copywriters are not solely responsible for knowing all of the regulations, of course, but experienced writers will know how to avoid possible trouble.

Copywriters need to cultivate enthusiasm and curiosity about their client and the products that are advertised, and they need to immerse themselves in the client's marketing arena to see what is going on among their clients' competitors. Being aware of trends and changing public attitudes gives copywriters the edge in creating new and exciting advertising that will capture the attention of the public. They need to know as much as possible about their clients' competition, what consumers are buying, and what "the trade" (retailers, clerks, salespeople, distributors, wholesalers, and agents) are thinking. In short, the copywriter needs to have a clear understanding of the environment in which the advertising will appear.

Copywriters should know their clients personally to become better acquainted with their ideas, their products, and their objectives. For the copywriter, being well informed is essential.

THE ART DIRECTOR

Like that of the copywriter, the job of art director demands talent, versatility, and the ability to adapt to many different tasks and situations. Besides being creative, the art director must be able to implement ideas and channel creativity. An art director has to think as well as feel. Without organization and the ability to work with others, an art director might come up with ideas that never get transformed to the printed page or TV screen.

The art director handles the visual side of the ad. Working in tandem with a copywriter and perhaps a TV producer (if the message is for television), the art director provides the visual message that the public sees first. The hot supermodel in an apparel ad and the action of a group of young people in a soft-drink commercial reflect the creative imagination of the art director. As always, teamwork is essential in the creative department, and an art director must be flexible and prepared to make changes when the team agrees that they are needed—even if the changes alter the art director's initial creative vision.

The art director's work is divided into three stages: conception, presentation, and production. First, a visual idea is conceived in the art director's mind, and it is discussed with others on the staff. Then, after modifications have been made, it is presented to the client. Finally, when the client approves the work, it goes into production. The art director is intimately involved with every step of this process, and his or her input is vital through the completion of the ad.

Art directors have a demanding job that often requires late hours and weekends to meet deadlines. In the case of TV commercials, art directors must frequently travel for on-location video production. For an airline starting new service to the Pacific, this might mean a week of production on a beach in Hawaii. Along with such occasional pleasantries, the job is filled with intense pressure.

Jobs in the Art Department

Traditionally, entry-level positions in the art department of an advertising agency or corporate advertising department include assistant art director and bullpen artist. Working in the art studio, or the bullpen, as it is commonly called, is something that every aspiring art director will experience before moving up the art department ladder. In an advertising agency, the art studio is the last stop before the artwork goes to the client. All creative work that calls for design or illustration passes through the art studio. Here, layouts and photos are mounted, headlines are changed, sample designs or "comps" are prepared, or a TV storyboard is constructed. One thing is for sure: working in the bull pen is never boring. This is where up-and-coming art directors learn their craft, master their skills, and work closely with more experienced art directors.

In the late 1990s, digital graphics technology began to influence the way agency art departments operate. Though many agencies still use pen, ink, marker, and pencil illustrations and film photography, progressively more preproduction work is created using computer graphics software such as Adobe Illustrator and Photoshop and digital cameras. In the twenty-first century world of advertising, computer graphics skills are essential, though the old-fashioned ability to draw clearly and accurately complements technology. Many agencies still employ staff or freelance artists to create illustrations or television production storyboards "on the fly" during brainstorm sessions and then rework the material digitally for client presentation.

The higher up you move in the art department, the more conceptual and less hands-on your job becomes. The next position up from assistant art director is junior art director, also a job that entails both design and production. The junior art director has more responsibilities than the assistant art director and works more closely with the art director.

The art director and senior art director are responsible for supervising the staff and creating and approving the ideas for the actual ads and seeing that these ideas are implemented by the rest of the art department. Quality control is the highest responsibility of the senior art directors, and it is not unusual for junior staff to see their hard work dumped for not meeting the exacting standards of high-level art directors.

At this level in an advertising agency, senior art directors have more contact with the client and the client's advertising department and more interaction with other departments in the agency.

The top position in the art department is executive art director. This person runs the art department, oversees all employee and budget matters, and is often an active participant in client presentations. Though much of this position is administrative and supervisory, the executive art director works on the conceptual part of all of the more important advertising campaigns.

The salaries of art directors parallel those of copywriters at similar levels. As with copywriters, salaries start low and increase quickly as one moves up the ladder. Advertising is an extremely popular field among artists. U.S. Department of Labor statistics show that more artists work in advertising than in any other field.

What It Takes to Be an Art Director

Art directors have special skills and talents, just as writers do. Some are best at designing print ads, while others may excel at writing television commercials. Art directors who work on print ads should be adept at organizing elements of type and illustration so that they appear clear, uncluttered, and easy to read and motivate the reader or viewer. The print ad must be effective in getting the advertising message across quickly and accurately. Art directors must have an extensive knowledge of typefaces and sizes and how they contribute and influence the readability of the ad. To see how important this knowledge is, look through any magazine and see for yourself how some ads are more appealing and readable than others. Successful ads are the result of an art director who understands what works, both technically and conceptually.

Art directors also need to have a sense of what visuals will make the greatest contribution to the effectiveness of the finished advertisement. Should the visual be a photograph? A cartoon? A drawing? Should it be black-and-white or full color? Whatever it is, should it be bold or soft? The way an art director responds to these questions can have a profound effect on the final product and its effectiveness.

Once the decision as to the art form has been reached, the next step is to decide which artist or photographer is best suited to produce the desired effect. Larger agencies sometimes have art buyers to handle this task, but in most cases, art directors perform this job themselves.

Training in art school or a school of design is a definite plus for those seeking this type of work. It is imperative that art directors be able to draw or sketch well enough to clearly demonstrate to the client how the finished ad will look, even though a freelance illustrator may be employed to create finished artwork.

The design of a television commercial is also in the hands of the art director, but the producer generally controls the decisions relating to the visual makeup of a commercial. Again, a team is involved that must work together to ensure that the highest-quality commercial is produced. Many of the same principles that apply to quality print ads apply to quality TV ads, and the art director must be adept at creating striking visuals, both on the printed page and on the screen.

THE BROADCAST PRODUCER

The TV spot producer is responsible for the creation and production of the television commercial. The producer must coordinate all parts of the project—the concepts, the people, and the technology. The producer does not usually contribute specific concepts for the commercials, but has a great deal of influence over the final form of the commercial, from initial budgeting to technical production. The producer's expertise is primarily technical, but involves a serious financial sense, as budgeting can be the difference between "go" and "no go" from a client.

Working with the art director and copywriter, the producer takes care of the many details involved in casting and shooting a TV commercial and often contributes new ideas to the production. In this regard, a spot producer must be familiar with all of the sound and video tools and aware of their potential and limitations. For example, most television commercials are now produced using digital video and sounds, but, occasionally, a producer and art director will still propose film for a unique look and feel that contributes to a product image.

Usually, the copywriter and art director approach the producer with an idea in the form of a storyboard. By looking at the storyboard, the producer can determine the logistics of producing the idea and whether it is practical and effective. When it is decided that the project can be done, the producer hires a production crew, a director, and a casting director. The producer is also responsible for staying on budget and must make sure that the project is completed on schedule and that the client is happy with the final results. The job entails a great deal of contact with people and, as usual in the advertising business, long hours and unpredictable work schedules.

Whereas art directors doing print ads have a limited range of design alternatives, producers have available all of the processes and devices of video and sound recording—animation, superimposition, close-ups, long shots, fade-ins, fade-outs, computer graphics, claymation, stop motion, slow motion, on-location filming, and a host of other optical tricks and special effects. The experienced producer is familiar with the entire range of techniques and knows which will enhance the persuasiveness of the ad's message while still adhering to the project's budget.

The production of TV commercials is an art form calling for talent and imagination on the part of those involved, particularly the producer. The best commercial producers will have a preconceived idea of the desired effect before shooting begins. Experimentation can occur on the set, but it must be limited by the budget, and it is the producer's responsibility to make sure that things do not get out of hand financially.

Spot producers also help decide on the jingle, sound effects, and background music that may be used in the commercial. And the producer works with the casting director to select actors and perhaps animals for the production.

The importance of the casting director in the production of TV commercials cannot be overstated. Casting directors screen applicants for parts in commercials and select those who appear best suited for the environment and message of the commercial. Casting directors generally keep files on available talent and know the talent agencies in town and the actors they offer. Casting directors must be proficient in the field of television to be able to evaluate the appearances, mannerisms, and voices of performers as they relate to the style and purpose for which the commercial is being produced.

Jobs in the Production Department

The entry-level position in the production department is production assistant. The production assistant, who works long hours for little money, helps the producer with all the details of the production. The junior producer, or associate producer, is given rudimentary production work, including test commercials and radio spots. The junior producer works more closely with the producer than the production assistant and of course assumes more responsibility than the production assistant. With experience comes the promotion to producer and the opportunity to oversee the production of full-fledged TV commercials. The salary levels for producers fall slightly below those of copywriters and art directors at comparable levels.

THE CREATIVE DIRECTOR

The creative director in an advertising agency is the guiding force behind the creative output of the agency. He or she is an experienced advertising professional with the necessary talent and innovation to spearhead the entire creative staff. This position is arguably the most culturally influential of all jobs available in advertising. Sometimes the creative director is the head of the entire agency. It is a highly visible position that has been held by many "legends" in the advertising business, including the previously mentioned Bill Bernbach, famous for his innovative ads for Avis, Alka-Seltzer, and Volkswagen in the 1960s. Another well-known creative director is David Ogilvy of Ogilvy & Mather. He began his small agency in 1948 and turned it into one of the largest agencies in the world, now part of WPP Group.

The creative director is responsible for the success of the advertising campaign. Creative directors are intimately involved with all aspects of the makeup of ads and must be knowledgeable about all of the areas in the creative department, including copywriting, design, and audio and video production. The creative director must pull together the best team of writers, art directors, and producers and maintain a consistently high level of productivity and creativity. The creative director in many ways is a cheer-leader in encouraging staffers in the department to boost creativity and productivity and must also cultivate new talent to keep the creative output fresh and current.

A creative director must also have a good head for business, as the position calls for participation in the running of the agency. Budgets must be managed, and the day-to-day business needs of the agency must be administered to maximize the agency's profits. The creative director must also be acutely aware of clients' needs and objectives, for often the client turns to the creative director for assurance and intelligent decision making during the development of an advertising campaign. As a result, the creative director must be articulate and capable of selling the agency's recommendations.

Most creative directors start out in the art department or as copywriters. It is in these positions that budding creative directors show their talent and ingenuity by creating successful ads and demonstrating leadership capabilities necessary for promotion to the higher agency ranks. The climb up the ladder can be tedious or fast, depending on the progress would-be creative directors show early on in their careers. Some rise to creative director in as little as five years; it is possible to reach this position before the age of thirty, as the advertising business is quick to recognize young talent.

The rewards of being creative director are great—both personally and financially.

THE CREATIVE PROCESS

Understanding how an ad is put together from start to finish will help you understand how creative services work as a unit and will help show the importance of the team concept at work in most agencies.

Print Advertisements

Copy
Although it is nearly impossible to separate the importance of the copy in a print advertisement from that of the artwork, good copy still remains the backbone of most successful ads. When first presented with the challenge

of a new campaign, the copywriter must be sure to understand the objectives and strategy behind the advertising. This knowledge is essential if the copy is to sell the product effectively. The creative director will often provide direction and guidance in this area. The copywriter will often work closely with the client's advertising department to ensure the client's satisfaction with the direction of the advertising campaign.

Next, the copywriter may develop several headlines or leading statements for the ad that highlight the primary selling points of the product. This is the stage where the slogans that so often become associated with a particular product are created. In some instances, copywriters prefer to write the headline and then the copy; in other instances, the copy is written first and the headlines are derived from the body of the copy. The headlines, of course, are the most prominent and most visible part of the print ad. A good headline or slogan will both convey the message of the product simply and clearly and grab the reader's attention. Many headlines are witty, based no doubt on the theory that if it is clever, you are more likely to remember the message.

Design

While the copywriter is working on the written material, the art director is developing the visual part of the ad. However, the order of this procedure varies; sometimes the copy is based on an existing visual. Often, the design is influenced by the direction of the headline, so the artist may not begin work until at least the headline of the ad has been developed. Once an idea has developed on how the ad should look based on the campaign strategy and preliminary copy, the art director develops rough layouts showing where elements of the ad are positioned in what will ultimately be the final version of the ad. The layout includes a rough drawing indicating what the photographs or illustrations will look like, where the copy and headline will be placed, and the location of any other components, such as logos, symbols, or disclaimers.

Comps and Mechanicals

Once the layout and copy have been reviewed and approved within the agency, the copy and a more carefully prepared version of the ad, called a "comprehensive" or "comp," are shown to the client. This process can involve a staged presentation or may be handled informally, but one way or the other, before any more work is done on the ad, the client's approval is necessary. Once the client approves the comp, the next step is the preparation of a "mechanical," or dress rehearsal–like design of the ad.

A mechanical consists of all the elements of the ad placed in exactly the position and size they will appear in print. In the era before digital production, mechanicals were assembled in a step-by-step hands-on process. The art department first typeset the copy in the style and size indicated by the art director, often using an outside firm that specialized in typesetting. However, with new computerized typesetting and other digital production tools, many agencies have in-house facilities. The next step is having the copy proofread by an in-house proofreader for possible mistakes. While this is taking place, the photo or illustration has been created and is placed on the layout of the mechanical. If the illustration or other portions of the ad were to be done in color, the colors are indicated on sheets of tissue that overlay the ad.

Today this process has been simplified and accelerated, using digital production tools that allow type, digital graphics, and photography to be assembled in a single layout on a computer monitor and colored by computer. Though the production process has become computerized, the essential creative process remains the same and must be conducted with the same step-by-step care.

Broadcast Advertisements

Up to a point, the processes involved in putting together a print ad and a TV or radio commercial are very similar. The advertising strategy and plan are identical, but the ad itself and the medium in which the advertising appears are different. Instead of headlines and copy, the copywriter must develop a script. And rather than a layout, the art director, together with the producer, begins work on a storyboard for the commercial. The storyboard resembles the panels in a long comic strip, and many agencies employ artists with a background in comic illustration to assist in the creation of storyboards.

Scripts

A television commercial script is divided into two parallel portions. On the right side of the page, the copywriter indicates the sounds that will be heard during the commercial, including all spoken dialogue, music, and sound effects. On the left side of the script, the writer indicates the visuals that will appear on the screen when each sound is heard. For example:

Visual	*Audio*
Dog eating dog food out of a bowl that bears client's logo.	*Announcer:* Make your dog a happy dog. Feed him America's favorite dog food.

Many of the same rules for writing effective advertising print copy also apply to writing scripts for television commercials. The opening statement should be brief and attract the viewer's attention. Situations should be believable and simple so that the story line of the commercial does not interfere with the ad's goal—to sell the product! Furthermore, the scriptwriter/copywriter should remember that in a TV commercial, the visuals carry more than half the weight of the ad in the audience's mind. The text should support rather than dominate the commercial.

Design

As with print ads, the design of a TV commercial is generally created after at least a preliminary script has been approved. At this stage, the art director and the copywriter prepare what is called the storyboard. A storyboard is exactly what it sounds like—a series of drawings mounted on a board, showing the action that takes place in the commercial. The number of frames in a storyboard varies from approximately eight to twenty, depending on the complexity of the commercial. The audio portion of the commercial plus instructions on what the visual portion should look like are printed at the bottom of each frame. The storyboard serves as a guide to the actual shooting of the commercial. It is in this form that the client first gets an idea as to what the final commercial will look like and can make the decision as to whether to go ahead with the project.

Production

Once the script and visuals have been approved by the client, production begins. Spots using live actors are most common. Commercials using animation, special optical effects, and other production specialties are handled by specialized professionals.

The first step in the production of a TV commercial is for the director of the commercial (either an employee of the agency or an outside expert hired to direct the spot) and the art director to begin casting the commercial. Actors who generally fit the descriptions of the characters in the commercial are auditioned and hired. Animals, if necessary, are screened and hired. Next, sets and outside locations are determined and the necessary permits obtained. All props and wardrobe, including a supply of the product to be advertised, are gathered together. The director and the agency then decide on the technical personnel needed for the production. Camera operators, lighting and sound technicians, makeup artists, hair stylists, and stagehands to move scenery and heavy equipment are needed to produce even the simplest commercial.

On the day of shooting, light and camera crews may spend several hours setting up and lighting the set. During this time, the director may coach the actors on their lines and map out the action that will occur in the commercial. Long delays are common during the video process, owing to changes in lighting and rearranging the set between scenes. In the end, shooting a thirty-second TV spot can take an entire day or more, and producers generally contract for twelve- to fifteen-hour shooting days.

Postproduction

In the postproduction phase, the many pieces of video and sound created during the shooting are assembled to begin the process of forming the finished commercial. The film is edited into its proper order, and the sound is synchronized with the visual. Recorded voices, music, or sound effects are added at this point. After a final review by the agency and the client, the film editor completes the final (or answer) print of the commercial. The film is then duplicated and sent to television stations, which will carry the commercial.

Creating an ad, no matter how brief or simple it may appear when you see it in a magazine or on TV, requires the efforts and cooperation of many people in creative services. These people must work as a team to produce quality work on schedule and within budget. Teamwork is the key to a successful advertising campaign.

CHAPTER

3

ACCOUNT SERVICES: PUTTING IT ALL TOGETHER

Perhaps more than anyone else, the account executive serves as the conduit between the client and the departments of the agency, such as media, creative, research, and production. The people who service the agency's clients can be thought of as the center around which revolve all other people in the agency. Account services coordinates the activity of all of the agency departments and is responsible for making sure that the client receives the best possible work and the best possible service. Account services also makes sure that the client's account continues to grow in billings and profits.

The account executive must be personable and articulate and must have a good head for business. He or she must know sales and marketing and—most of all—must be able to sell the client on the creative work of the agency. Enthusiasm and knowledge of the client's products are important characteristics of successful account executives. An account executive must motivate and encourage agency people as they work for the client and must be able to resolve any conflicts and differences that arise. Good people skills are essential for anyone hoping to be a successful account executive.

Along with the client and the client's advertising department, the account executive formulates the approach of the advertising campaign, identifies any marketing weakness, and looks for the best strategy to increase the client's sales in the future. The account executive works closely with the people at both the agency and the client's marketing and sales departments to pinpoint the marketplace for particular products and to determine the demographics and psychographics of the type of consumers likely to buy the products. Together with the media department of the agency, the account executive makes certain that the client's money is spent effectively and efficiently. Account services also works in tandem with the creative department to ensure that the client's wishes are taken into account in the development of the campaign.

THE DIVERSITY OF AN ACCOUNT EXECUTIVE

The functions of an account executive are demanding and diverse. It's fair to say that no two days are alike. To excel in account services, an individual must combine sound business judgment, a high level of proficiency in advertising, and the ability to interface well with people. An account executive's responsibilities fall into five main categories: planning, coordination, presentation, regulatory matters, and agency profit management.

Planning

The account executive plans the advertising with the client and others within the agency. Together, they decide the goal of the advertising—that is, the ideas that are to be communicated. They define the audience to be reached and appropriate media to be used, the money required, and the standards for measuring advertising effectiveness. The planning stage is where the foundation and execution of the advertising campaign are determined.

To establish a sound advertising plan, the account executive must become knowledgeable in the client's business. He or she must know the sales and profit goals of the client, as well as what the client's competitors are doing and if they are succeeding and why. All these factors are important in the planning stage.

Because account executives must deal more and more with economic, statistical, and financial concerns, an increasing number of advertising account executives have graduate business degrees in marketing or business administration. Previously, account executives were known for their social skills and salesmanship, but as advertising has become more of a science, more and more good account executives are recognized for their analytical skills.

Coordination

Because an agency's work is the product of the efforts of many different specialists and departments, it falls on the account executive to make sure that all of the elements of the agency's output are brought together on time and consistent with the objectives of the campaign. The account executive must oversee the work of the creative people, media specialists, producers, researchers, production and traffic, and, often, outside suppliers. All of this means that the account executive needs to have a thorough working knowledge of each area of the business. The account executive essentially serves as liaison between the agency and the client.

The account executive must be a good judge of copy and must be able to keep the advertising presented to the client on track and consistent with the client's objectives. The account executive must understand art and layout in order to judge material to be presented to the client. In short, a good account executive must be imaginative and a sound critic whom colleagues respect. He or she must be tactful in the evaluation of the work of coworkers and must persuade people that suggested changes are justified. A person in this position will avoid compromise and yet keep everyone happy.

The account executive must recognize the strengths and weaknesses of various forms of media and be able to convey this knowledge to the client. This means being able to articulate the reasons why magazines or television may be best for a client's needs.

The account executive needs to be up-to-date on production requirements for broadcast and print media and the costs and time factors involved in all areas of production. He or she must be familiar with research sources and techniques and must understand their applications. If the campaign calls for point-of-sale displays or special packaging, the account executive must know the sources and what will work best.

Finally, and most importantly, the account executive must know and understand the people within the agency—the members of the agency team—and must be sensitive to the pressures connected with their jobs and be able to motivate and stimulate these people to do their best work. The account executive is like a football coach, leading and inspiring a team of professionals to reach a defined goal.

Presentation

The account executive is usually responsible for presenting the agency's work to the client. When an advertising campaign is under way, the account executive will have frequent informal meetings with the client to discuss details relevant to the campaign and to present new commercials or written copy for approval. The matters discussed in these meetings may include the extension of media commitments, analysis of the budget, and changes in copy and layout. When the time comes to present a new plan or campaign, especially one that departs from the course that has been followed, the presentation is likely to be more formal. In such instances, the presentation will explain the reasoning behind new ideas and proposals and show samples of new layouts and concepts. There are apt to be a number of client representatives present at this meeting who are not normally involved in the day-to-day advertising decisions.

The account executive is responsible for organizing and staging the presentations. It may be a formal presentation with slides and flip charts, or it may be a low-key discussion around a conference table. The proposed advertising can be in final finished form, or it may be in rough layouts or storyboards. Consideration is given as to how many agency people will actively participate in the presentation and what role they will play. Will the creative director or art director join the meeting? What about the copywriter? This aspect of the account executive's job is a little like being a theatrical director or producer. A winning presentation is often determined by the thoroughness and excitement created by the presentation and the effectiveness of the presenters.

Regulatory Matters

As mentioned in Chapter 1, there is a growing body of government regulations that control the content of advertising. The account executive must be familiar with this ever-expanding and complex body of rules and the codes and practices of publishers, stations, and networks. A good knowledge in this area will avoid regulatory problems that could interfere with the efforts of the agency and the client.

Agency Profit Management

In addition to the other duties and responsibilities, the account executive is responsible for the profitability of each account. Agency management will always be ready with reminders that the agency must attain its profit objectives. Every account must contribute to profit. Accordingly, the responsible account person will monitor the people power and time that each account requires. In return, a significant portion of account executive compensation may be based on bonuses derived from account profitability or media billings.

Other Responsibilities

Beyond the work that involves the development of strategies and new campaigns, the account executive takes care of the day-to-day business of the account. Account executives spend time getting to know the client and collecting new information and insights into what makes that client happy. It is equally important for the account executive to have a good idea of what is going on at the client's company.

The account executive is also responsible for scheduling, making sure that ads are completed and scheduled in the media on time. Though other agency departments handle much of this work, account services is ultimately responsible if an ad is late or incorrect.

Account executives also have more than their share of paperwork. This generally includes contract reports, which are summaries of the communications between the account executive and the client. These reports include records of telephone calls, correspondence, and accounts of meetings and presentations. Writing reports and summarizing meetings is time consuming, but the information is essential to keep track of points that were agreed on. With the dozens of changes that an ad can go through during production, it is crucial to know who said what, when, and to whom.

An effective account person will balance the need to concentrate on details with the need to keep in mind the goal of the campaign. Too much emphasis on memos and meetings can stifle the creative side, and too little attention to details can make for a confused and ineffective campaign.

Writing is a significant part of an account executive's work. This writing can include presentations, internal memos, letters to the client, and reports on meetings with the client. A great deal of information passes from the agency to the client and from the client to the agency, all through the account executive. The account executive who writes well becomes an effective communicator for the agency. Unlike copywriting, this writing is not creative but must sell the agency's ideas to the client and represent the client's position to the agency. A clear, concise, persuasive writing style that incorporates the technical and intuitive sides of advertising is desirable.

Account executives with out-of-town clients can expect to do a great deal of traveling. Often, when TV commercials are involved, the account executive may be away from home for as much as a month at a time. For some this is a hardship, but others may view it as an exciting part of the job.

JOBS IN ACCOUNT SERVICES

The jobs available in account services are diverse and challenging, as you'll see from the descriptive "tour" that follows, from the entry-level position of assistant account executive all the way to the top—account director.

Assistant Account Executive

This position is the entry-level position in the account services department. It is a good place to view the inner workings of the agency and to learn from the more experienced account executives. The assistant account executive's responsibilities usually involve considerable paperwork and legwork. The job calls for office administration, execution, analysis, compiling statistics, conducting studies, keeping records, and monitoring myriad details. It also entails the need to attend meetings and seminars and basically to support the work of the agency staffers.

In some agencies, though, an assistant account executive may start out working as the key agency contact on smaller accounts or on one brand or product within a large account. For example, an assistant account executive might be given full responsibility on a breakfast cereal account for a new variation of an old brand or a new cereal package that will have its own campaign. The assistant account executive also must learn what people in other agency departments do and how this work relates to the client. All this information must be assimilated quickly for the assistant account executive to function effectively. Often, just when the assistant account executive is comfortable with an account, he or she is switched to a different account. Frustrating as this may be, such moves are often required to serve the changing needs of clients and will give the fledgling account executive a broader base of knowledge and skills for the future.

An assistant account executive usually reports to one account executive. At some agencies, the assistant is put through a company training program preparatory to beginning work on specific accounts. Each agency tends to have its own program for the training and advancement of employees in account work. It often takes a few years to be promoted to account executive.

Account Executive

The next step up the ladder in account services is the position of account executive. As expected, this job is less administrative and more conceptual than the job of assistant account executive. More time is devoted to working directly with the client and the client's advertising department. Like the assistant account executive, the account executive gains knowledge and experience through working with the client and other departments in the agency, but the account executive's involvement is deeper and the responsibility greater.

The account executive is generally the key person on any given account and carries the responsibility of maintaining contact with the client to the degree that is necessary to ensure that the client's needs and wishes are serviced properly. The account executive's day usually includes meetings with agency people in such departments as creative or media and phone conversations or meetings with the client. As noted earlier, detailed records must be kept of all contacts, and the account executive is responsible for overseeing this record keeping.

Usually, the account executive deals with tasks and problems as they occur during the course of the day. The job entails constant changes and a great deal of unpredictability.

Account Supervisor

The position of account supervisor is the next step up from account executive. Generally, the account supervisor handles two to four different products or clients. The account supervisor spends less time worrying about details and more time in supervision and is likely to have a staff of two or three account executives. Therefore, the account supervisor must be familiar with the work of these staffers and have the ability to delegate and oversee such work.

In this supervisory capacity, the account supervisor is increasingly aware of the big picture within the agency. Lessons learned on one account will be applied to another. The account supervisor has a greater influence on the overall success of the agency.

Of course, the more experienced an account executive becomes, the less supervision is needed. At that point, the account supervisor can devote more energy to conceptual account strategy. Like the account executive, the account supervisor maintains a close relationship with the client's advertising department and often is involved at the highest level of corporate management.

Management Supervisor

Continuing the climb up the account services ladder, on the next higher rung is the management supervisor, who has control of two or three account supervisors. Often, a management supervisor will oversee several major products from a large client or several different clients. The management supervisor is less involved in the day-to-day business of the client and more involved in campaign strategy and helping the client arrive at major marketing decisions.

Management supervisors work closely with high-level management and the director of the client's advertising department. They are also responsible for the profitability of each account and how these accounts benefit the agency. The management supervisor will study account budgets, review major creative work and major marketing reports, and make sure that the agency staff is functioning efficiently.

Account Director

Many of the larger agencies have a position that ranks above management supervisor—account director. The account director may be in charge of one or two big accounts, including all products and brands, and will have two or three management supervisors on staff. The person in this position is heavily involved in managing the agency and developing new business, as well as overseeing the business of account services. In rare circumstances, an agency will have a position above account director—that of group account director. The group account director supervises the account directors in the agency.

Profitability is the cutting issue in most agencies in today's tough economy. In a move to cut costs, some agencies have eliminated certain layers of management, leading to a doubling up of responsibilities for those in account services. But in addition to profitability, the employee structure of an agency is determined largely by the agency's size and the number of accounts it handles.

CHAPTER

4

MEDIA SERVICES: FINDING THE RIGHT AUDIENCE

The media services department in advertising agencies has grown in importance in recent years. Before television and radio, there were not many media specialists. But today, with such a growth in communication technology and with the high cost of space in print media and the Internet and the high cost of time on television and radio, media selection has become a science.

For advertising to sell a product or service effectively, it needs to be read, seen, or heard and acted upon by the right audience. Regardless of how good the advertising is, if it does not reach the proper people, it is worthless. This is where media services takes on the responsibility of evaluating, selecting, and recommending the publications, stations, and programs that will carry the advertising to the widest possible effective audience. And since clients pay to advertise in these media, media selection and media buying command great attention in the client-agency relationship.

Consider the powerful presence of network television, the many specialized cable networks, satellite broadcasting, and the increasing number of magazines and specialized and local newspapers, and you can readily understand that media experts are important and in great demand. As such, opportunities in media services continue to grow. These people play a major role in the strategic planning of advertising campaigns and the operation of advertising agencies.

FUNCTIONAL COMPONENTS OF MEDIA SERVICES

Media services serve three major functions: evaluation, selection, and buying. Let's take a closer look at each of these areas and how they interface within the operation of media services.

Media Evaluation

People involved in evaluation are called *media planners*. They are responsible for developing the media plan, which is the result of evaluation and selection of media known to be viewed by the client's audience. This process begins with media research. Every agency, regardless of size, has a research library, and large agencies subscribe to a great many different research services. These services supply data on reading, viewing, and listening habits, as well as profiles of readers and viewers attracted to specific publications, TV and radio programs, and even outdoor billboards. In addition, planners need basic information on media, such as advertising rates, deadlines, and mechanical specifications.

For decades, the primary sourcebook for basic information on newspapers, magazines, radio, and television stations has been *Standard Rate and Data Service*, now incorporated as *SRDS Media Solutions*. Separate editions of SRDS are published to provide information on newspapers, consumer magazines, business magazines, radio, and television. The information includes circulation and viewer data, costs of various units of print publication space or broadcast time, frequency discounts, and markets served by each media outlet.

For many years, SRDS was considered the only reliable source of media information, but the service neglected other demographic information that media planners needed to make their buying decisions, including audience age makeup, incomes, lifestyles, and buying habits. Other media services, including Nielsen Media Research, Arbitron, Mediamark Research Inc. (MRI), and Simmons Market Research Bureau (SMRB) now provide this type of more sophisticated market information. The Nielsen and Arbitron rating systems provide a wealth of statistical information about TV and radio audiences that is extremely valuable to the media planner. SMRB and MRI both measure the demographics of magazine readers. They also supply supplemental data on newspapers, radio, and television and general consumer information on product usage and consumption.

The companies conduct regular national surveys of twenty thousand adults from which demographic, marketing, and media information is assembled. Other services measure psychographics, analyzing people's lifestyles and interests, likes and dislikes, attitudes and beliefs, prejudices, and patterns of use of one product over another. The media planner will use these resource tools to conduct a successful media evaluation and provide a solid media plan.

By using these resource tools, a media department can give a manufacturer like General Motors or Honda some assurance that its new-car advertising is aimed at the right type of buyer. Until quite recently, it was very hard to have any degree of assurance about such distinctions, but computerized databases have greatly increased media planners' ability to analyze and apply multiple sources of information.

In today's agency, the computer is the cornerstone of media research and selection. Consider an advertiser with a large budget and an advertising plan specifying the use of magazines and network TV to reach women between the ages of twenty-four and thirty-five years old. The media planner needs to reach the greatest number of these women the greatest number of times. The media planner assembles a list of magazines and television time slots that are likely prospects for attracting a high concentration of the target audience and submits the list to the assistant planners.

The assistant planners then use media-planning software and various database information to project the probable audience results for various combinations and presents alternative plans for media mix, audience "reach," and cost.

Media planners also maintain extensive files of other media data in the agency's media research library. This information includes media kits obtained from publication and network sales representatives that describe in detail their audience characteristics, circulation, and results of surveys conducted by the media. In an effort to complete the picture of the value of their medium, most publications now routinely survey their audience about their buying practices, product interests, and business and leisure activities to supplement the media data services.

Media planners are more than just keepers of these records. They must be able to evaluate this material and decide what is reliable and relevant. This skill requires that they understand the techniques used to collect their data and whether such procedures are valid. They make the final decisions about which research services the agency will buy or subscribe to and the extent to which these services will be used. Their job requires an analytical mind that finds statistical investigation both fascinating and challenging.

Media Selection

Media selection is the job of putting together a recommended schedule using the available information. This is done in the most precise way possible and by combining media that will be read, heard, or viewed by those people most apt to respond to the advertiser's product or service. This task begins with an understanding of the advertising plan—the audiences to be reached, the requirement for repetition, the length of the advertising message, and the money available to carry out the task. This understanding is fundamental to making intelligent choices. Media selection is initially the responsibility of the media planner; it is subsequently reviewed by others in the agency.

Network TV is far and away the most popular medium for advertisers of general consumer products, obviously because of the huge numbers of people that can be reached.

The first step in media selection is to single out one or more categories of media that are suited to fulfill the objectives of the advertising campaign. From that point on, the planner, with the assistance of the research team, selects the markets, stations, programs, and time and days of the week for radio and TV ads and the publication dates, size, and often position of magazine and newspaper ads. Everything is tailored to a precise schedule. Equally important is the job of juggling dollars and insertion dates until they fall into place in a fine-tuned schedule. Owing to knowledge and creativity and a good understanding of available media, the process of media selection is scientific and accurate.

From 1990 to the present, one of the fastest-growing areas in media is cable television, which has been slowly eroding the dominance of broadcast network television. In recent years, the media planner has begun to regularly include cable television as a key component in media plans and acknowledges the narrow audience targets of such networks as MTV and VH-1 for young audiences, Black Entertainment Television for African Americans, Oxygen for women, and Spike TV for men.

If the media plan calls for radio advertising, selection of powerful general-audience stations may be important if the advertised product is for the mass public. However, if the product or marketing message targets males, advertising on a radio station broadcasting local baseball may be the best choice. If the advertiser wants to reach teenagers, the media planner might choose stations featuring pop music.

When selecting magazines, the media planner must be acutely aware of the demographics of audience and the readership. A media planner would typically not place an ad in *Playboy,* for example, to reach women. This may be obvious, but in other cases extensive research is needed to determine which magazines are best for a particular product or service. Advertising in magazines has a longer life, and with so many titles to choose from, the media planner can generally find special-interest magazines that pinpoint ideal readers for the advertised product. With the increase in the number of specialized titles, magazines are playing a larger role in the schedules of many national advertisers.

Planners involved in media selection continually meet with the sales representatives of specific media to learn more about competitive situations and changes within the media. To stay up-to-date, they must spend considerable time meeting with these media advertising sales representatives and assessing the validity of their data and comments.

Good media planners must be analytical and comfortable with figures, imaginative and well informed, interested in the broadcasting and publishing businesses, and alert to the importance of the intangible (or unmeasurable) aspects of each medium. As in every other advertising job, planners must also be eager to find innovative ways to do their work.

Media Buying

Media buying is the next step. Buying advertising space in a magazine or newspaper is relatively easy, since most publications have unlimited space for sale. It is, however, not so easy in the case of radio and television time, particularly television spots on top shows. For example, there is a limited number of spots to be sold on the annual telecast of the National Football League Super Bowl, and advertisers of automobiles, beer, and other male-oriented products scramble to be first in line. Often, preference is given to those advertisers who purchase time throughout the year and to those advertising agencies that are big TV spenders. Generally, media buyers are given the specifications, such as dates, markets, and audience demographics, against which they must find the best spots for the advertiser's purposes. They then determine from the sales representatives what spots are available—known in the trade as "avails."

With this information in hand, buyers will negotiate for the purchase of the avails that best meet specifications and budgets. Because the rates quoted by most broadcasting stations are quite flexible, purchasing is truly a matter of negotiating, and professional and knowledgeable buyers will stretch the client's budget substantially through skillful negotiation.

The local television stations and national networks stand firm on rates for top shows and prime-time slots, but for spots on the late, late rerun at 2 A.M. of a 1970s sitcom, there is considerable flexibility in rates. Frequently, buying is done on the basis of oral commitments that are later confirmed in writing. For this reason, it is absolutely essential that both buyers and sellers live up to their agreements scrupulously.

The best buyers are good at detail; they are effective data analysts who work well under pressure. When things get busy at the agency, buyers are even busier. It is work that calls for a special skill in negotiation and persistence. A buyer who does well is often moved up to a position in media supervision or a more senior management job, although some people choose to make a career of media buying and can do very well financially.

Within advertising agencies, media personnel spend a tremendous amount of time with sales reps from the media. Such representatives may be employed full-time by the media (such as the major networks, which have their own staffs); or, in the area of broadcast, they may be employed by an independent representative organization. These salespeople receive training in the demographics and buying characteristics of the viewers and readers of the media they represent so that they can assist the advertising agency's media personnel in assembling and evaluating the data required for their media recommendations.

The most active media buying occurs in the area of broadcast. The peak season for network TV media buying is in early May, when the networks announce their fall TV schedules, and the buying activity lasts through the end of July or August. Buyers must be knowledgeable about the new and returning shows and their content and appeal. Unlike print buying, where the rates for advertising space are fairly well set, broadcast buying is a constant game of wheeling and dealing. The variability of rates is greater and the money spent can be enormous. Broadcast buying is more demanding than print buying, though print buying calls for its own special kind of expertise. In buying space in magazines and newspapers, there is rate flexibility for the big advertiser. In addition, negotiation centers on preferred positioning of the advertisements in the magazine, special treatment in merchandising, and, in the case of less successful publications, editorial support for the advertiser.

EXECUTION OF AN EFFECTIVE AD CAMPAIGN

People in media services need to be able to work well with other departments in the agency and with clients. Input from the client is invaluable to the success of a media plan and should be actively encouraged. Interaction with other agency departments occurs on a daily basis and is of great benefit to the media department. Here's how media services work hand-in-hand with other agency departments to execute an effective advertising campaign.

- *Creative services.* Media service employees interact with creative staff to keep them apprised of the latest developments in media audience and demographics or surveys obtained from media sales representatives. Media services staff are on the lookout for new developments and attempt to measure the impact on the media plans for the clients of the agency. Media services staff advise the creative staff about alternative media, such as billboards, transit cards, online services, and perhaps even skywriting.
- *Research.* Media services use the research department to provide analyses of demographics and other statistics that influence media buying. The research department is an important source for information on population shifts and other geographic changes. It also provides information on competitive activity.
- *Account services.* As previously noted, account services is the representative of the client to the agency and vice versa. It is vital that media services personnel interact well with account services, as these people are responsible for coordinating the overall advertising plan and for making the client's wishes known to other agency departments.

JOB OPPORTUNITIES IN MEDIA SERVICES

Assistant Planner

The typical entry-level position in media planning is that of assistant planner. In this job, an entry-level employee gathers statistics for media planners and becomes acquainted with the basic research tools discussed earlier in this chapter. An assistant planner will spend considerable time working with facts and figures and will gradually begin to understand the meaning behind this information and how it influences the media plan. This research and statistical work provides the media planner with the materials to develop a full-fledged media plan.

Junior Buyer

On the media-buying side, the entry-level position is known as junior buyer. Like the assistant planner, the junior buyer is mostly involved in working with numbers, spreadsheets, and lots of paperwork, scheduling, and placement. It is a position where an employee learns the basics of media buying. It is the first step to becoming a media buyer. This training period is necessary and usually does not last more than a year or so.

Junior buyers earn about the same salary as assistant planners—the bottom of the advertising agency scale.

Media Planner

As previously noted, the media planner is responsible for media evaluation, media selection, and development of the media plan. He or she will work with the information gathered by the assistant planner and suggest a definite plan for the client. Usually, a media planner will have had at least two years of experience in the media department before being elevated to this position.

Media Buyer

Media buyers buy space in print and time in broadcast media. Besides negotiating media buys, these people track budgets and schedules and provide postanalysis reports. Junior buyers usually graduate to the position of media buyer faster than assistant planners graduate to the position of media planner.

Media Supervisor

Normally, a media supervisor will have worked as an assistant planner and as a media planner before being stepped up to this position. A good knowledge of those positions is a requisite for this job. This position involves a great deal of overseeing and providing guidance to planners and assistant planners and a lot of contact with the heads of other agency departments and the client's advertising department.

Broadcast Supervisor

The broadcast supervisor coordinates the buying operations of the media department. In this position a person serves as supervisor to the buyers and junior buyers and usually negotiates the larger and more difficult buys. The broadcast supervisor ensures that the department work is completed as scheduled. A person in this position must be intimately aware of everything that is taking place in the broadcast industry as well as current trends and all the happenings in broadcast programming.

Associate Media Director

This position calls for more involvement with the administration of the agency and the agency's long-term projects and goals. The associate media director works with planners and buyers as well as with the client and other agency departments, especially account services. Often, this position carries the title of vice president.

Media Director

The media director is the head of the entire media services department. This person has the responsibility of making sure that all planning and buying move along smoothly for the benefit of the agency and client. The media director makes sure that the staff is of the highest professional standing and that all staffers are working to the best of their abilities. An employee in this position can expect to hold the title of senior or executive vice president in the agency and to play an important role in shaping agency policy and growth. Generally, the media director is heavily involved in presentations for new accounts and will often be included in important meetings with top clients.

CHAPTER

RESEARCH: DEFINING THE CONSUMER

Today, the trend in agency research departments is away from statistics and demographics and toward cultivating a better understanding of the consumer. The researcher may use one-on-one interviews, psychological profiles, analyses of attitudes and behaviors, and psychographics (the psychology or motivation behind consumer actions) to get to the heart of the question, What is our consumer like? Advertising research is about people—their likes and dislikes, their attitudes and beliefs, their lifestyles and buying habits and perceptions of the marketplace. Researchers try to find out not only what people are buying but why they buy it. It all comes down to understanding people and human behavior—what makes people tick. Data are important, but what the data tell us about the people behind the data is more important. In a nutshell, the research department can be thought of as the representative of the consumer within the advertising agency.

The warm, comfortable, person-to-person ads that appear on TV these days can be looked at as a product of this approach in advertising research. By better understanding the people who purchase the client's product or service, the research department can better help the client to reach out to more consumers and increase sales. Researchers develop strategies based on their findings that help the agency and client work toward the goal of increasing sales. The primary responsibility of the researcher is to identify the buying consumer for the client.

The research department works closely with the creative department and with the client's advertising and marketing departments. Though many researchers fall into particular specialties, such as consumer studies, media research, market research, and copy testing, more often than not today's research department is staffed with generalists—those who can handle all areas of research and consequently focus on the needs of a single account. This way, the researcher becomes extremely knowledgeable about a specific account and is better able to respond to problems and offer solutions.

METHODS AND RESOURCES

The research department looks to two basic areas for data: original and secondary sources. Original research is that which is conducted by the research department itself. The direction of this research is decided by the client and the research department and can include interviews in shopping malls, telephone surveys, mailed questionnaires, computer analyses, and the hiring of outside research firms. Secondary research can be defined as any outside data that help define consumer trends and behavior. Secondary sources include magazines, newspapers, independent studies, books on consumer attitudes, corporate studies, or anything that the agency or client did not specifically commission. Often, the client has its own research department that works in tandem with the agency's research department.

VALS and Consumer Behavior

One of the ways of looking at consumer behavior is by means of the VALS categories, a psychographic method. VALS, which stands for values and lifestyles, is a system of categorizing the consumer according to psychological type. This system was created by SRI (formerly known as the Stanford Research Institute). VALS are divided into four categories:

1. *Need-drivens:* those with limited financial resources who are driven more by need than choice
2. *Outer-directeds:* those whose buying habits, attitudes, and activities are influenced and shaped by what they think others will think
3. *Inner-directeds:* those who live their lives according to inner values rather than the values of others

4. *Integrateds:* those whose inner direction and outer direction are combined into a functional entity

Researchers work to determine where the target audience falls for a particular product or service in the VALS spectrum. This knowledge can be extremely helpful to the planning of an advertising campaign.

Market Simulation Testing

Another valuable research method is market simulation testing or test groups. A test group of consumers are shown advertising for a particular product and then are taken to a mock store, given script to represent money, and asked to shop. Researchers can determine how effective the advertising is by how many of the respondents "buy" the product. Many times this procedure is repeated a few weeks later to determine whether the test consumer will purchase the product again. This test is useful in helping the agency and the client decide if the product is worthy of introduction into the marketplace.

Market Research

Market research is more often undertaken by the advertiser, but it is frequently carried out by the agency research department or by a specialized research firm. Market research, the basis of modern marketing decisions, involves determining what areas of opportunity are open to a manufacturer and what kinds of packaging, pricing, distribution, and promotion will make the manufacturer's product successful. The following is a list of the major information sources utilized by market researchers:

- Government statistics, an incredible source and readily available and free to everyone
- Trade, business, and industrial magazines that serve specific fields
- Business statistics assembled by various trade associations and business groups
- Client information, which is the private and often closely guarded property of the advertiser

- Syndicated services that provide information on the movement of an advertiser's goods and those of competitors on the retail market. Without these services, it is very hard to tell what is happening to products after they leave the factory. This is particularly true in the case of packaged goods, such as cosmetics, prepared foods, and drugstore items.
- Visits to the "trade," which involve going into the marketplace to find out what dealers, retailers, and salespeople are doing to help or to hinder the sale of an advertiser's product. This kind of investigation is of particular value when a number of competitive products are sold in the same store. Salespeople can have a strong influence on the sale of products based on their own preferences.
- Specially commissioned private research that gives readings on the attitudes and behavior of various consumer groups. This type of study is valuable when the manufacturer is not too clear about consumer attitudes but knows that they are important to successful marketing.

THE SKILLS OF A SUCCESSFUL RESEARCHER

Those who expect to succeed in the field of research need to be analytical and have a natural curiosity about people. They should feel comfortable with numbers and be able to interpret data, but extensive training in mathematics and statistics is not necessary. Attempting to understand the many variables of human behavior is the best training a researcher can hope to have. This type of knowledge is gained through life experience and is invaluable to the researcher.

An ability to search for and find pertinent information is requisite for a job in a research department; researchers use many sources in their work, and it is necessary to sift through a great deal of information to get to the information they need for their current project. Researchers must be enthusiastic followers of trends and developments in consumer attitudes, opinions, habits, and lifestyles. They should also be clear and persuasive communicators, both orally and in writing.

People in research must continually ask themselves how they can use their findings to help increase the sales of the client's product or service. Researchers may find themselves working closely with the client's marketing department to find new ways to increase a product's visibility and market penetration. By combining their efforts, these two departments can offer strong support to any advertising campaign.

JOB OPPORTUNITIES IN RESEARCH

Research departments are generally smaller than other agency departments, and many agencies contract much of their research needs to independent research companies. Many of the positions named here are found only in the larger ad agencies, and these positions vary greatly from agency to agency.

Project Director

There are two levels of project director in the research department—junior project director and senior project director. The position of junior project director is considered the entry-level position. Project directors focus their energies on gathering facts and background information without analyzing the information. Being able to organize the data in a way that senior researchers will understand and interpret is the mark of a good project director. Project directors are involved in writing questionnaires, coordinating surveys, and conducting one-on-one interviews. Project directors also need extensive knowledge of computer tools, including spreadsheet and database software, Internet search engines, and proprietary information databases such as Lexis-Nexis and DIALOG.

Research Supervisor

This position, sometimes referred to as research account executive, is the next level up from project director. The person in this job begins to assume supervisory responsibilities. Along with coordinating the more complicated research studies and writing research proposals, the research supervisor keeps an eye on the project directors and assigns their work. The research supervisor is more involved with specific research studies for the client and therefore has more contact with the client than the project directors.

Associate Research Director

The next step up the research ladder is the position of associate research director. Agency employees in this position are expected to have at least ten years of experience in research. These employees work closely with the client and other agency departments, especially creative services and account services. Associate research directors supervise the activities of outside research firms hired by the agency and the activities of their own research staff.

Research Director

After about fifteen years in research, a research department staff member may be promoted to the position of research director. An employee in this position is usually a specialist in a particular area of research. The research director is responsible for assigning work to staff members and maintaining a productive working environment. As the head of the research group, this person represents the department to the client and has more say in the agency's direction as a whole.

Executive Research Director

Some of the largest agencies also have the position of executive research director—the absolute top of the heap. This person has research directors on staff and usually is involved in the management of the agency. Most of the work in this position is supervisory.

C H A P T E R

6

OPPORTUNITIES IN TRAFFIC AND PRINT PRODUCTION

In some advertising agencies, print production and traffic are combined into a single department; in others, they are separate. Regardless of the arrangement, these departments work so closely together that it is often difficult to determine exactly where one leaves off and the other begins. Needless to say, print production and traffic are extremely important to running a smooth and efficient advertising agency.

TRAFFIC

This department can be likened to the air traffic control tower at an airport. It is the department in which timetables and deadlines that govern an agency's activities are monitored. Traffic is responsible for seeing that all of the elements of an advertisement or commercial are fitted together and forwarded to the designated medium in the proper form and on time. The material can range from type and illustrative elements needed for print advertisements to audio transcriptions for radio commercials.

Traffic is a matter of coordinating, obtaining approvals at each stage of the ad's development, meeting deadlines, and seeing that everything goes smoothly and according to plan. Traffic people help others in the agency do what they should when they should. Directing the flow of work in and out of the agency and between various agency departments is the heart of the traffic department's responsibilities. Like account services, traffic falls in the middle of the action at the agency and thus is usually considered a stepping-stone to a position in account services.

Deadlines are probably the most crucial part of a job in traffic. Each publication has its own deadline for ad placement. Missing a deadline can seriously hamper an agency's advertising plan, especially if the ad must run at a certain time (for example, in a Friday newspaper for a weekend sale). Fortunately, good traffic staff are extremely thorough and conscientious and rarely miss deadlines. Often, traffic staff work closely with each other to avoid mistakes that contribute to missing deadlines.

Directing Traffic: What It Takes

Good traffic planners need, above all, to be orderly and well organized. They need to be able to manage a great amount of detail accurately. They must know about the processes that are involved in the creation of an advertisement and understand the amount of time needed to complete each step. They must be able to track and manage multiple projects at one time. Patience and quick thinking come in handy when directing an advertising agency's traffic.

Traffic employees must also be able to deal effectively with outside suppliers and with members of the creative team at the agency. They must know which creative people respond to coaxing and which ones need to be shaken up to get them to meet deadlines. Meeting deadlines often depends on the traffic person's ability to push others to complete work on time. A certain amount of finesse is essential in this job.

Traffic work can be demanding, but for those who enjoy it and do it well, it provides the satisfaction of knowing that you are part of the indispensable lubrication for the agency's gears.

PRINT PRODUCTION

Print production is responsible for ensuring that a print ad appears in a newspaper or magazine as planned—on time, in place, and within the budget. To meet these responsibilities, the print production department is also responsible for buying the services that go into the printed material produced by the agency, including advertisements, pamphlets, brochures, outdoor posters, flyers, sales manuals, and direct-mail material. The print production staff also deals with technicians, printers, graphic service companies, and freelance artists. As a result, production employees maintain source files of available facilities for each of these services and must know the strengths and weaknesses of each supplier. Having a good rapport with suppliers can be beneficial when deadlines are tight; suppliers may make special accommodations for production staff they know well. Print production works together with the art director to see that the art department's ideas are properly reflected in the final ad. The production person brings to the artwork the technical expertise that the art director may not possess. This collaboration between production and art director often results in a successfully executed and effective print ad.

A print production worker must be knowledgeable about photo reproduction processes, both the latest digital photo editing and production tools as well as the older photoengraving processes still in use for some advertisers—particularly those that use high-quality magazine media. These processes affect not only how the artwork will ultimately look but also how much it will cost to produce. Among the older photo production and printing processes are offset, rotogravure, and halftone gravure (a kind of combination of offset and rotogravure). When these processes are used, the production supervisor will usually ask for bids from a few engravers, choose one, and then see the job through to completion. Print production people must always keep up on the latest production trends and technical advances. A strong general knowledge of print production techniques is essential for a person working within this department.

Typesetting

Typesetting was once a special art within the advertising field, and some of the bigger agencies had typography managers and a typography staff. Like the production supervisor, the typography manager worked with the art director but dealt with type size and style. Once the art director and typography manager decided on type size and style, the typography manager was in charge of reviewing bids from typographic services. Today, most typography is computer generated, and digital production processes give art and production directors thousands of typefaces or "font" options for their ads. Graduates of college design programs are now educated in typography design as well as their creative applications.

The art of typography is far from dead. Art directors may choose to have unique typefaces designed specifically for their ads and to make a particular font part of the overall image. The art director may want to re-create a particular design used in product packaging and turn it into a print advertising font. In these cases, print production staff may have to work with type designers or calligraphers to produce the unique design sought by the art department. For example, comic book–style lettering in "word balloons" have become a popular graphic technique in advertising art, and while much of this kind of type production can be done using computer software, art directors may contract with a freelance letterer with comic book experience.

Budget Control

Another area of responsibility for print production is budget control. Print production employees need to know whom to contact to get the job done on time but at a good, competitive price. In most cases, it is necessary to get competitive bids, particularly on large or complicated assignments, and of course it is required on all government contracts. This requirement usually means added time and almost always requires extra paperwork.

Like those in traffic, good print production people need to be well organized and capable of giving close attention to the details of a number of projects that must be processed simultaneously. The production employee must also know the amount of time each supplier needs to complete a job under normal circumstances, as well as the absolute minimum time each needs under the most urgent pressure.

Both traffic and print production can be career jobs for those who find this sort of work satisfying and rewarding. For the most part, however, they are learning jobs that serve as training for better-paying positions in an agency, usually in account services.

As an important aside, in the past, almost everybody in an advertising agency started in one of these jobs. This is no longer true, but it is essential that account people, writers, and designers understand the nuts and bolts of print production and traffic so that they can cooperate and contribute to the smooth operation of the agency.

Art Buying

The buying of art is closely related to print production. In most agencies, art buying is a section within the print production and/or traffic department. In some agencies, it may be a separate department.

Buying artwork demands knowledge, good taste, and negotiating ability, as well as the ability to understand the needs and objectives of creative people, especially the art director, for whose output the art is being purchased. There are many parallels here to the job of casting director for a broadcast production. The art buyer must have extensive information about the talents of a varied number of commercial artists—from photographers to illustrators to cartoonists. Buyers must also know who is best qualified for fashion and who is best for industrial products. As a result, art buyers need to keep a database, not only of specialties but of subspecialties as well.

Art buyers are also constrained by deadlines and must know who among the various artists or photographers is available to deliver on time and who is too busy to meet a required deadline. Buyers are also governed by budget considerations and must be able to deliver the quality of work required at prices that are acceptable to the client. In carrying out these tasks, good business judgment and a keen negotiating skill are a must. Art buyers must be sufficiently well organized to keep their records in order to make the job run smoothly and professionally.

Art buying is a fascinating and gratifying occupation for anyone who has a true appreciation of the whole spectrum of commercial art and who enjoys dealing with interesting and talented people, gets satisfaction from discovering new talent, and enjoys helping aspiring young artists.

JOB OPPORTUNITIES IN TRAFFIC AND PRINT PRODUCTION

Traffic Assistant

This is considered the entry-level position in traffic. The traffic assistant reports to the traffic coordinator and is responsible for handling departmental paperwork, looking after details, and keeping an eye on deadlines. A college degree is not required for this position in the contemporary agency but may be essential for promotion and advancement into other departments.

Traffic Coordinator

The traffic coordinator is the person who takes care of the actual shep-herding of an ad as it makes its way into print. A person in this job can expect to have constant contact with the creative and account services departments. Some traffic coordinators also work closely with the client and the client's advertising department.

Traffic Manager

The traffic manager oversees the entire traffic department, including scheduling, supervising staff, and controlling the agency's print ad activity. Traffic managers see to it that their staff members are working well together and responding to the needs of the agency. Budgets and person-nel matters are also the responsibility of the traffic manager.

Production Assistant

This position is the equivalent of traffic assistant, but on the production side. Production assistant is the entry-level job in print production and includes many of the basic duties found in this department. The produc-tion assistant reports to the production supervisor and handles a good deal of the paperwork. Again, a college degree is not necessary to break into this department but may be necessary for future career advancement.

Production Supervisor

This position is print production's equivalent of traffic coordinator. The production supervisor, sometimes called the buyer, is the person who actually deals with the suppliers and negotiates prices.

Production Manager

The person in this position is considered the head of print production. The production manager assigns work to the staff and ensures that all the work being done is up to professional standards. The production manager works closely with the heads of other agency departments and with the client to ensure that the best print work is being done in the most cost-efficient manner possible.

AGENCY MANAGEMENT AND ADMINISTRATION

In any agency, someone has to be in charge and someone has to attend to the administration of profit and loss and business operations. This chapter discusses the important role of agency chief executives and the functions of the agency administrative departments—financial management, legal services, personnel, office management, and various other support groups. Administration may not be as glamorous as other aspects of advertising, but there are many interesting and challenging positions within the structure of an advertising agency's business operations. And administration may be the path to the highest salaries and greatest perks.

AGENCY CHIEF EXECUTIVES

The air is thin at the top. Only a few talented, hardworking men and women reach the pinnacle of agency chief executive. Natural leadership ability is a requisite for these positions, and these people have risen to the top because they demonstrated their leadership talents all the way up the ladder. Though the job of chief executive is demanding, the financial rewards are great; many chief executives earn over $500,000 a year, along with equity participation, options, and generous perks.

No one department of an agency has a monopoly when it comes to grooming chief executives. A look at the chief executives of many of the top agencies today will show that these people came from creative services, account services, media, and research. Leadership is found in many different areas of the advertising business, and those with natural leadership ability will rise to the top regardless of where they begin their careers.

Agency chief executives have the responsibility of ensuring the agency's organization, finances, and output are achieving excellence in all aspects. Filling key management positions, assisting the client in building business, and taking care of long-range planning are all the responsibility of the chief executive. At the largest agencies, the chief executive is often responsible for overseeing worldwide operations. Traveling also plays a large role in the life of the chief executive, especially in an agency with many branch offices. It is a position that demands a great deal of physical energy and stamina.

A chief executive must be good with people and know how to get the best work from the agency's management staff. Being good with people also pays off when dealing with clients.

The chief executive is expected to be in personal contact with important clients, and the clients generally look to the chief executive for reassurance and counsel on many matters, including improving their business and getting the most from their advertising.

It may seem that all of these responsibilities are too much for one person, and, indeed, there may be more than one person at the top of an agency. Many of the larger agencies have an executive team that runs the agency and an executive committee that provides direction on important decisions. For example, the executive team may include a chief operating officer (COO), a chief executive officer (CEO), an executive creative director, and a chief financial officer (CFO). Generally, there is an agency president, and frequently there is a president for international operations. A liberal use of important-sounding titles also helps in client contact, as it enables the agency to parade high-level executives around the world to meet with clients and prospective clients.

The executive committee may also include senior staff from each of the agency's departments. These committees act as a sounding board for the executive officers and will meet regularly to discuss problems, opportunities, and agency objectives.

At a small agency, the one or two people at the top are usually the owners or major partners. In such instances, one or two people are responsible for the major management decisions at the agency. Regardless of the arrangement, agency chief executives are the people who call the shots and influence the success or failure of the agency.

FINANCIAL MANAGEMENT

The main function of the finance department is to see that money comes in on time and bills and other obligations are paid on schedule. An agency's cash flow, and ultimately its profit, is what keeps it in business. Therefore, the finances must be well managed. Also, financial responsibility in client relations has become an important issue in the post-scandal era of the twenty-first century, and maintaining appropriate financial records subject to client audits has become critical.

Every agency places an enormous amount of space and time with the media each month. This places a great demand on the cash flow at the agency. Generally, clients are billed when space and time are ordered. As a result, the agency should receive payment from the client before the bill is received from the media.

If there is a breakdown in this arrangement (for example, a slow-paying client), the agency can find itself in a cash crunch. Therefore, managing cash flow at an agency is important. The finance department also manages the agency payroll and often supervises company employee benefits, such as medical insurance, profit-sharing programs, and retirement plans.

At many of the larger agencies, the finance department is divided into two principal areas—media billing and production billing. Those who work in media billing invoice clients for the cost of ad space and TV or radio time and pay the media promptly. In typical production billing, expenses for each job are recorded as soon as they are determined, and after the work is completed, the people in production billing prepare invoices for review by the account services staff. There are many elements of expense in a production bill, and those involved with this work must be able to track the details and organize the billing. In some agencies, media billers work in the media services department and production billers work in production and traffic rather than as a separate staff in the finance department.

Most agencies have at least one person who is responsible for monitoring cash positions and for ensuring prompt collection of bills and prompt payment of supplier invoices. The larger agencies have both a treasurer and a controller to assume these responsibilities. They, in turn, are backed by clerical, secretarial, and supervisory personnel with qualifications the same as those for similar jobs in any other business.

Agency Compensation

Among the most critical of an agency's financial management matters is agency compensation. Today, most agencies are paid a fee for their work. This fee may be paid on an assignment-by-assignment basis, where the cost of the work of completing each ad or series of ads is billed separately. In other cases, agencies work according to a defined contract. The client and the agency agree that the agency will perform specific tasks over a given period at a specified cost. The cost of each individual ad and the production charges are billed to the client, but the cost is not to exceed the amount agreed on in the contract. Agencies sometimes are asked to bid on a project, such as a new catalog, and will then contract to complete the project for no more than the stated sum.

Agencies are also compensated in part by charging an add-on charge for materials or services bought from outside suppliers—artists, photographers, printers, film producers, and other independent operators. The usual add-on for these outside purchases is 17.65 percent of the supplier's charges, which translates to 15 percent of the total amount billed to the client. This amount generally compensates the agency for the cost and provides some profit for performing such services. Furthermore, fees are often charged for publicity and speech writing, sales promotion work, staging and conducting sales meetings, and any other service that the agency may perform.

In most cases, the agency receives and retains a commission of about 15 percent (or sometimes a bit less) when paying media for space and time placements. The exceptions include retail ads in newspapers and other "noncommissionable" media. If a full page in a magazine costs $1,000, the publication bills the agency $850. The agency bills the client the $1,000, the amount the client would have to pay if dealing with the media directly, and retains the $150 commission. The amount retained by the agency provides income to the agency and may be the only income the agency receives from the client. In other cases, the client will pay the agency an additional fee. In the case of a large user of commissionable space or broadcast time, the client may insist on a rebate of a portion of the commission or require that the agency perform certain services in return for keeping the large commissions. As the advertising business has become more competitive, it is now quite common for large advertisers to negotiate media commissions with their agency. For example, a large client may allow their agency to retain 12 percent and expect rebates or other services to make up the difference between that 12 percent and the 15 percent commission the agency receives from the media.

Keeping track of agency compensation and its complications and exceptions is the responsibility of the finance department.

LEGAL SERVICES

Because laws and regulations affecting the advertising business are in a state of constant development and refinement, most large agencies have one or more lawyers on staff to serve as advisers to the account services and creative services personnel.

These lawyers must review the advertising that the agency produces and make sure that it complies with the laws, rules, regulations, and customs that govern the advertising industry consumer protection laws and the general laws of copyright and trademark. They usually review the first draft of ideas through the finished product. Lawyers also handle litigation, real estate and leasing matters, contracts for outside suppliers and performers hired for commercials, and essentially any legal matter in which an agency may be involved.

Agencies that specialize in serving clients in highly regulated industries, such as pharmaceuticals or securities, are more likely to have larger legal staffs. Agency attorneys also serve as a link to whatever outside legal counsel an agency may employ.

Advertising agency law is highly specialized, and although there are few job opportunities in the field, it can be fascinating and challenging because of the formative nature of the rules that govern the advertising business.

HUMAN RESOURCES

Human resources management, formerly called "personnel," is another important department in an advertising agency. Human resources staff manage the business of employment—posting positions, conducting interviews, administering employee records, and managing compliance with myriad state and federal regulations regarding employment discrimination, immigration, and personal leaves.

Besides handling applicants for employment, human resources staff also manage the employee health and dental plans, vacations, retirement plans, and other employee benefits. Human resources can also be involved in staff training programs and in helping to maintain and boost employee morale.

OFFICE MANAGEMENT

As in any business, office management is essential to the smooth operation of an advertising agency. The office manager is responsible for all of the day-to-day decisions that can make the workplace enjoyable and efficient or disjointed and chaotic. Specific responsibilities will vary, depending on the size of the agency, with office managers in smaller firms generally handling a wider variety of tasks with greater responsibilities.

SUPPORT SERVICES

Like other businesses, agencies need secretaries, typists, clerks, receptionists, librarians, and information technology specialists. As advertising agency offices have evolved into a digital, paperless environment and information technology has become a critical component of operations, an agency may need programmers, analysts, and computer support staff. Although the tasks involved in advertising support positions are similar to support positions in other businesses, the atmosphere is likely to be more lively and challenging.

CHAPTER

8

THE CORPO-RATE SIDE: ADVERTISING AND BRAND MANAGEMENT

Throughout this book, there have been references to corporate jobs in advertising. Now it's time to take a closer look at these opportunities. There are two areas in which people can build a career in advertising within corporations—advertising management and product, or brand, management. Career opportunities in both of these areas will be discussed in this chapter. But first, let's see how corporate advertising management differs from advertising agency operations.

CORPORATION VS. AGENCY

There are plenty of differences between working in an advertising agency and working in a corporate advertising department, but the most obvious is the corporate culture. The agency environment tends to be loose and casual, fostering the creativity that drives advertising creation. The corporate environment is more conservative and structured, supporting broader management goals, sales projections, and other aspects of corporate management.

What kind of work environment do you want? Consider the differences as you examine your career options within advertising. In the final analysis, your personality and your long-term ambitions will determine where you are most likely to be comfortable.

The corporate environment tends to be more rigid and mapped out in terms of job levels and advancement. Corporate job descriptions are often detailed and very specific. Corporate advertising tends to be heavily administrative, a branch of the corporate marketing operations. Fiscal reports, budgets, market surveys, and evaluation of advertising campaigns play a big part in the day-to-day activity of the corporate advertising employee. The higher you move up the corporate ladder, the farther you are likely to move away from advertising and the more toward broader aspects of corporate management and business strategy.

If you want a lifetime in advertising, creativity, and media production, the corporate advertising department may not be for you. However, you will certainly see more and learn more about all aspects of business by working within a corporation. Your career goals will influence your choice.

There are some attractive incentives in working on the corporate, or client, side of the advertising industry—higher pay to start and more control over the direction of the advertising outcome. Jobs in corporate marketing and advertising tend to pay about 20 percent more than comparable jobs in advertising agencies, especially at the entry level, and this can be an attractive inducement. But perhaps the most significant difference between the corporate side and the agency is that when you are paying for the advertising, you are in control of its direction. The agency works for you.

One of the toughest jobs for advertising agency staff is their overwhelming need to please their clients. As one agency old-timer said to a group of young account services employees, "Remember the golden rule: He who has the gold makes the rules."

Agencies live in constant fear of losing clients. A morning's mail—in print, E-mail, or voice mail—can carry enough terminations from clients to wipe out an agency and all the jobs that go with it. So if you are seeking job stability, you need to focus on the corporate side of the business. Working on the corporate side eliminates the frustration of having to worry about client approval of your ideas and plans.

Decision-making power is ultimately in the client's hands. If you enjoy the power of directing the advertising and don't mind the burden of administrative work, a career on the corporate side may be for you. Look at it this way: if advertising is your first love, work in an agency; if you are a businessperson at heart with an interest in advertising and marketing, build your career on the corporate side.

Keep in mind that people move back and forth between the agency side and the client side, so it is possible to try both areas and see which one suits you best.

CORPORATE ADVERTISING DEPARTMENTS

Corporate advertising departments offer attractive opportunities for a lifetime career in advertising. The corporate advertising department sets advertising policy for the company, establishes advertising goals, makes sure that the advertising prepared by the agencies is consistent with the company's sales and marketing objectives, and keeps these agencies up-to-date on product development, research, market conditions, and top management's current thinking and concerns. The corporate department is the conduit between the agency and every department of the client company.

The advertising department is held accountable for the agency's performance and for the quality and effectiveness of the advertising. The advertising department usually has the power to approve or disapprove the agency's recommendations and ideas. Though the advertising department can usually reject an advertising recommendation proposed by an agency, in some cases approval or disapproval may come from the marketing or sales department or at higher levels of corporate management. The latter is much more common in companies in which advertising plays an important role in the success of the products. Examples would include the fields of packaged foods, fragrances and cosmetics, fashion, and soft drinks. By contrast, in businesses such as financial institutions, engineering services, and manufacturers of heavy machinery, decisions on marketing and advertising are generally left up to the experts who head these product lines.

In some companies, the advertising department has the authority to hire and fire agencies; in others, it can only recommend such action to corporate management. It is fair to say that the more important the advertising is to the success of the company's products, the more often top management is heavily involved in such decisions.

In companies that have more than one agency, the advertising department carries the responsibility of directing and coordinating the work of the different agencies. The department must make sure that advertising for each product is consistent with company goals and image. Also, corporate media contracts must be coordinated and maintained to ensure that a given issue of a magazine does not carry too many advertisements for the company's products while the next issue carries none. The advertising department also must make sure that all media scheduling is organized for the lowest possible rate and maximum impact. Most media offer rates that reduce the unit cost when six, twelve, or more advertisements are used by one advertiser in a given year.

The advertising department also controls the budget, which includes expenditures for time and space, production, and the internal costs of running the department—payroll, travel, telephone, supplies, rent, and utilities—everything that is chargeable to the department.

Many advertising departments create and produce their own direct-mail material and brochures, catalogs, packaging, and point-of-sale material, although this work is sometimes done by an agency or specialized outside supplier. It's part of the function of the advertising department to keep the work in harmony, directed toward the same company goals, and consistent in tone and approach.

Job Opportunities in Corporate Advertising Departments

The structure in a corporate advertising department differs greatly from that of an advertising agency. In small companies, the advertising department is generally managed by an advertising manager with the help of one or two assistants. In large corporations, the advertising department is likely to be headed by an advertising vice president or a director of advertising, who presides over separate advertising units, each under the direction of an advertising manager. In some companies, the department has its own research unit; in others, there is a separate research department that assists the advertising department.

Though advertising departments are set up differently than agencies, they employ similar kinds of people, often with identical qualifications and background. Although the work may be similar, the big difference, as noted earlier, is that the advertising department can make the important final decisions and can commit the corporation's funds.

Some corporations have established house advertising agencies whose structures, jobs, functions, and specialties are similar to those of an independent advertising agency. The only difference is that they work for just one client and are usually physically housed on the premises of the corporation and paid by the corporation. Because the people who work in these house agencies are on salary like other company employees, they are less concerned with profit and loss than are the employees of independently owned agencies.

BRAND MANAGEMENT

Brand, or product, management is the other principal area of corporate advertising and in recent years has become one of the dominant fields of marketing, often driving advertising development. Brand management is usually part of the marketing or sales department. The brand manager concept was established in the 1930s by the giant packaged-goods corporation Procter and Gamble and has since been adopted by many companies, particularly those that manufacture food, packaged goods, and many different products and brands.

Corporations that use the brand management system assign one person to a specific product or product group. This executive, often with his or her own staff, handles all the work that needs to be done to advertise and market this product. In many ways, each product is treated as if it were a separate company or "profit center"—a kind of company within a company. In addition to advertising and sales promotion, the brand manager's responsibilities can include marketing strategy, business planning, profitability studies, and market research. Coordinating the advertising is only part of the job of the brand manager, but an important part. The life and death of a product can depend on the effectiveness of the advertising.

The brand manager works closely with account services and the creative services staff at the corporation's advertising agency. In the early stages of an advertising campaign, the brand manager plays a crucial role in interacting with the agency. From the brand manager the agency gets a handle on the direction and goals of the client in regard to advertising for that particular product. Brand managers are heavily involved in the development of ideas presented by the agency early on, and later they may sit back and let the agency work its magic, checking on the work periodically to make sure it is in line with the company's objectives.

Success in brand management, though, has more to do with being a good business executive than being able to create advertising. A brand manager is really a strongly oriented marketing person, running a business within a business, selling one product—with the advertising being one facet, albeit an important facet, of the business. A person in this position is also involved with product development, product improvement, packaging, marketing strategy, and a host of other details that evolve in the course of selling the product. This job is for someone with a talent for marketing and business and a head for advertising. If this sounds like you, brand management could provide you with a challenging and rewarding career and a stepping-stone to top-level corporate management.

To prepare for a career in brand management, a job seeker usually needs at least an undergraduate degree in marketing or business administration, and to rise to the ranks of vice president, most will need a masters in business administration with a concentration in marketing or advertising.

RETAIL

National retailers like J. C. Penney, Wal-Mart, or Target provide another source of jobs outside of the advertising agency. Most retailers do their own advertising and rarely hire outside agencies. Because the bulk of their advertising is done in-house, talented professionals are needed to create and execute advertising for these retail marketers.

The world of retail hires a wide variety of advertising professionals, including copywriters, TV producers, art directors, media people, research people, and even traffic managers. Since ads need to be produced quickly and frequently, often designed to tie in with sales and in-store promotions, the advertising staff must be able to organize and maintain an efficient system of fast response to put together the necessary advertising. Because of the speed required in producing retail advertising, quality is sometimes sacrificed, but getting the ad placed on time takes precedence over the finer points of good design. People who like a fast pace and who can work quickly and enjoy working under great pressure and daily deadlines are ideal candidates for jobs in retail advertising.

All in all, opportunities outside the advertising agency are diverse and challenging. Often disregarded by those entering the advertising field, corporate and retail advertising jobs can lead to great personal and financial rewards that may not be found in advertising agencies. Remember to consider all the possibilities as you chart your career in advertising.

CHAPTER

9

WORKING FOR A MEDIA COMPANY

Media companies want to sell advertising space and time for their media properties. As a result, media companies use every imaginative, creative, and innovative device to capture the attention of the advertising community. This includes ads in the advertising trade press, sales presentations, analytical research, promotional premiums, and frequent direct-mail solicitations. Media firms are heavy users of direct mail because the ad agencies and advertisers whom they wish to influence are easy to identify and relatively few in number. This makes direct mail ideal for their purposes.

Working for the advertising department of a media company or working in advertising sales is another exciting opportunity in advertising. The advertising department of a media firm functions in a similar manner to the advertising department of a corporation. Because media companies need to use advertising to impress and influence advertisers and advertising agencies, there's a great emphasis placed on highly creative and high-quality work.

The function of the media sales department is to sell advertising space in their publications or time on their stations or networks to agencies and advertisers. As a result, these media representatives call on advertisers and their agencies and find themselves totally immersed in the day-to-day world of advertising—dealing directly with company ad executives and calling on agency media and account services executives. This selling is done on a one-on-one basis and through presentations to groups of agency and client executives. Such presentations often involve the use of sophisticated audiovisual devices to more accurately highlight the unique qualities of each medium.

Today, media sales is a growth field and a strong area of opportunity. Though the media industry plunged into a recession in 2001, it began to recover in mid-2003 as advertisers returned to bigger advertising budgets and mass media.

The two more important media sales categories are print (newspapers and magazines) and broadcast (radio and television).

SELLING SPACE IN PRINT MEDIA

Newspapers

The United States has more than fifteen hundred daily newspapers and seven thousand nondaily newspapers, designed for regional, neighborhood, religious, and ethnic audiences, among other demographics.

More than 55 million people each day read at least part of a daily newspaper. Most newspapers are at least 65 percent advertising and currently account for more than $7 billion worth of advertising a year. Newspapers made up approximately 19 percent of all advertising in 2001. The interest in advertising in a specific paper depends on the rates, circulation, market served, and number of people who read it regularly. Advertisers and agencies gather the needed data from sources such as *SRDS Media Solutions* and in discussions with newspaper advertising sales representatives.

Newspapers are the most timely of all print media because they are published so frequently—daily or at least weekly. Thus, a retail ad for air conditioners can appear the morning of a forecasted heat wave and a sale on snow shovels can be promoted before a predicted winter storm.

Most advertising appearing in newspapers is placed by local businesses. Sections within each newspaper attract advertisers whose products relate to specific editorial content. Thus, cake mixes are advertised in the food section, homes and home improvement in the real estate section, and fishing tackle in the sports pages.

Newspapers carry classified and display advertising. Display ads range from small ads to large full-page ads. Most display ads include illustrations. Classified ads, or "want ads," often advertise jobs, real estate, used cars, and private goods for sale. Used car and real estate classified ads may be large advertisements, but most classified ads are only a few lines and seldom contain illustrations.

Magazines

Magazines are visually more attractive than newspapers and are generally published to serve a specific, or target, audience. The editorial content of a magazine determines the audience it wishes to attract. Each magazine is edited to appeal to the needs, interests, or tastes of a particular cross section of the public. *TV Guide*, for example, is edited for people with an interest in television programming and TV personalities. *Time* and *Newsweek* are both current-events magazines; *Tennis, Golf Digest, Working Mother,* and *Electronic Musician* are even more specialized.

Advertising executives refer to these publications as consumer magazines. Magazines that provide information and guidance on highly specialized fields are called trade, business, or industrial magazines. Publications such as *Women's Wear Daily* or *Photographic Trade News* are classified as trade magazines because they deal primarily with the news and changes in their respective fields. Closely related are business publications, such as *Advertising Age, Adweek,* and *Creativity,* which serve the advertising profession, and *Editor and Publisher* and *Publisher's Weekly,* which serve the newspaper and book publishing business. Industrial publications are generally more technical and include titles such as *Electronic Products, Functional Photography,* and *Plastics Engineering.*

In addition to national magazines, there is a growing group of publications edited for local consumption. Such magazines on the consumer side include statewide publications such as *Texas Monthly, Connecticut,* and *New Jersey.* There are also successful magazines that cater to highly affluent audiences on a local basis, such as *Palm Springs Life* for the resort community in California and *North Shore Magazine,* which serves the wealthy suburban communities of Chicago. These local magazines are growing fast and are receiving more and more attention from national advertisers who need to advertise locally and prefer the more attractive appearance and environment of a magazine as opposed to a newspaper. Many national magazines have responded to this trend by now offering local metro editions that enable a national advertiser to place an ad in one or two local markets and not pay for the entire circulation.

More than $11 billion was spent on consumer magazine advertising in 2001—about 5 percent of all advertising spending. About $4.5 billion was spent in trade and business publications—about 2 percent of the total.

Print Media Sales

The guaranteed minimum number of readers that a magazine or newspaper will deliver is a factor determining the "base rate" for ad space in that particular magazine or newspaper. Unlike TV time rates, which historically have always been negotiable, print advertising rates historically have held firm; but the recent recession has changed the situation. Advertisers and agencies are now putting more pressure on media for price and merchandising concessions. Rates vary according to the size of ads and the frequency of appearance of ads in a given twelve-month period. An advertiser who will run a six- or twelve-time schedule receives a better rate than the occasional one-time advertiser. Positions with higher visibility, such as the back cover and the inside front cover of a magazine, as well as the use of color, may add to the cost, but frequently they are made available without a premium to lock up a pending sale. Also, since there is no limit to the available space that a publication can print, magazines and newspapers usually will try to sell as much advertising as possible.

Print media sales representatives, especially at magazines, must build their business with existing accounts and also develop new accounts. This is not as easy as it appears. A media representative needs to be familiar with all aspects of the advertiser's business and must be able to offer suggestions to the advertiser as to how to improve sales and increase market visibility through the use of his or her publication.

A media rep must take a personal interest in the client and build the client as an important advertiser. Acquiring new accounts is more difficult than maintaining existing accounts. A media rep really has to sell the quality and audience of a magazine to a new client and prove to the client that advertising in that magazine will be better than advertising elsewhere.

A great deal of information is gathered to support the readership of successful magazines and newspapers. The ages, incomes, educational levels, occupations, buying habits, car ownership, and other characteristics of readers all influence advertising buying decisions. This information will influence the advertiser in the selection of one magazine over another and is the subject of constant debate among advertisers, agencies, and the media sales representatives. Equally important is editorial quality and environment, trends in circulation, the overall appearance of the publication, and its standing among the competition. The media sales representative performs the important task of providing advertisers and agencies with this vital information.

JOB OPPORTUNITIES IN PRINT MEDIA SALES

Account Manager or District Manager

The account manager or district manager is an ordinary salesperson with a fancy title who sells advertising space for a publication in a specified geographic territory. The job calls for good old-fashioned sales work—maintaining old accounts, soliciting new ones, keeping up-to-date on accounts and competition, and making lots of sales calls. These representatives are the backbone of the media sales department, and the economic success of the magazine or newspaper is based on their performance.

Group or Regional Manager

The group or regional manager serves as supervisor or sales manager to a specific staff of representatives serving a defined geographic area or branch office. Generally, this executive double-teams with individual representatives on tough prospects, larger accounts, and difficult sales situations. A group or regional manager is usually a person with a successful sales record who has moved up a notch.

Advertising Director

The advertising director is the head of the advertising sales department. This person acts as supervisor to the staff and oversees all areas of the department, including promotion, advertising rate policies, forecasting and budgeting, and of course the direction and motivation of the firm's sales staff.

SELLING SPACE IN BROADCAST MEDIA

Television

By far the most visible and most controversial advertising medium is television. Since its beginnings around 1950, television has grown into the largest national advertising medium, with a revenue of nearly $39 billion for broadcast network television and $15.5 billion for cable TV in 2001. Network television commercials advertise products or services that have nationwide appeal and availability and that, for the most part, are financially within the reach of most people. By network TV we mean a number of television stations located in cities across the country that are affiliated with each other to carry the same program during a given time slot. Similarly, the same advertisements are generally shown with each program. Because of network television, each participating station can telecast a wider variety of shows of better quality than they might produce on their own. And advertisers are assured of program consistency as their message is telecast across the country.

Local TV is used essentially by retailers, automobile dealers, department stores, banks, and other local businesses and merchants. National advertisers also use local TV to hype a product in a given market or to serve a special competitive need or satisfy a seasonal or geographic market need. Spots may appear on locally produced shows or on nationally televised shows as local commercials.

Cable television offers a more selective advertising approach. Instead of choosing from among six broadcast network programming packages, viewers now choose from 100 or more channels specializing in news, sports, music, food, home remodeling, and other interests. Because of this diversification of programming content, advertisers can select an environment in which the advertised product is more likely to attract the most interested buyers. For example, a brokerage house will reach better prospects for its services on CNBC than it will on the Disney Channel.

A TV commercial may take the form of a thirty-second spot, often televised with another thirty-second spot to form a one-minute media purchase. "Partial 30" spots of ten and twenty seconds are also common. Spots of one minute or longer, once very common, are now rare. On most television programs, commercials are spaced at ten- to twelve-minute intervals. Thus, an average half-hour prime-time network program has a total of about nine and a half minutes of commercial advertising.

Advertisers, with input from their own advertising and marketing people and from their advertising agencies, are very selective in the shows they sponsor. Advertisers may select from sports events, comedies, dramas, or special events and will seek to create an atmosphere or setting that will successfully showcase the products they want to sell.

Radio

Although radio is primarily a local medium today, it reaches more people in more places and under more varied circumstances than any other medium. The majority of homes in this country have two or more radios. In addition, there are car radios, boat radios, portable radios, and radios with headphones for walkers and joggers. Today, automobile drivers and their passengers represent the largest segment of the radio audience.

Because of this audience power, radio is used by national and local advertisers to promote goods and services that appeal to the masses and that are widely distributed and readily obtainable. For example, discount retailers are heavy radio advertisers; Tiffany's is not. About 8 percent of all advertising spending—or about $18 billion in 2001—is spent on radio. Nearly 75 percent of this expenditure appears as local spot advertising.

Today, there are few network radio programs, so most advertisers who wish to use radio coast-to-coast do so by buying spots on a station-by-station, city-by-city basis or by buying time through the large sports radio networks, such as ESPN Radio, or national "talk" radio networks, such as ABC Talk Radio.

An advertiser can also be selective in choosing an audience that is more likely to be interested in the advertised product or service. For example, early-morning and late-afternoon broadcasts are listened to by people driving to and from work. Since these are heard by automobile owners, advertisers selling cars and products related to the interests of business-people are more likely to do well.

Another consideration is the selection of radio stations according to their programming. A station featuring country music will have a loyal and definitive audience that appeals to advertisers who identify with that type of consumer. Some stations aim at reaching special ethnic groups; others are aimed at identifiable age-groups and consumer groups. The products advertised on these stations are the ones likely to appeal to the tastes of such listeners.

Broadcast Media Sales

The big difference between selling space in print and selling time in a broadcast is that broadcast rates are highly negotiable and no two advertisers can be on the same station on the same program in the same exact time slot. The price of a ten-second spot will vary considerably, with a slot on the number one TV show costing more than a slot on a less popular show airing at an off-hour. And since the popularity of programming changes constantly, so do the advertising rates.

When local stations expect to sell time to national advertisers, they do so through national rep firms. These firms are located in major advertising centers, and they interact with advertising agency spot buyers. A rep firm can be thought of as the local station's agent, or representative, in the marketplace, or as the intermediary between the local stations and the advertisers. They help to match the station's available time with the advertiser's needs. Working for a radio or television rep firm calls for strong sales ability; not only must you sell the advertiser time, but you often need to sell or negotiate with the station to accept your advertiser's commercials in the time slots they want. Obviously, there is a lot of interest among advertisers to run their ads in prime slots and in conjunction with special events. Working for a rep firm is challenging and sometimes stressful work.

Often, in the network TV arena, bids are solicited by advertisers and/or agencies for time on a particular network, and the salesperson that can put together the best package for the advertiser will get the business. Sometimes, the advertiser will establish a set budget to spend on advertising and will ask a network to come up with the best possible package within the stated budget. The proposal will include pricing, time and dates, and the particular programs for the campaign. The proposal with the best mix of programming, price, and available time will usually land the business.

TV network sales is a huge business, but the number of positions in network TV media sales is limited. Getting a job in this area without a successful sales record is extremely difficult.

Media sales in the local market for local radio and TV stations is usually handled by the station's own sales staff. The local ads that run on these stations are negotiated and sold by the sales staff and usually run on local programs, though they sometimes appear in local slots allotted to the local affiliate on network or syndicated shows.

Besides the advertising sales staff, all TV networks and many individual stations have advertising departments that work at promoting advertising sales and building audiences. Either working in tandem with their own ad agency or working separately, these advertising departments handle the ads to promote the shows for a new season, promotions, and publicity. These advertising departments are not part of the media sales department. They offer an excellent opportunity to work in advertising with advertisers and with advertising agencies.

JOB OPPORTUNITIES IN BROADCAST MEDIA SALES

Sales Planner

This position is basically administrative and may include such duties as database maintenance, basic media research, filing, answering telephones, and reading and routing mail. It is a starting point for many people who want to break into the business.

Sales Assistant

In network TV and large stations, sales assistant is generally the next step up from sales planner. An employee in this position prepares proposals to serve the needs of advertisers. This job provides an excellent opportunity to learn how to prepare schedules and learn the industry.

Account Executive or Sales Representative

On a small station or at a rep firm, this is often an entry-level position. This is typically the only sales job you can land right out of college, as other broadcast sales jobs usually require experience. Account executives and sales representatives negotiate and sell the broadcast time. They have heavy contact with advertisers and advertising agencies. An account executive must be acutely aware of what is happening day to day with the network stations and with competition.

THE QUALITIES OF A GOOD MEDIA SALES REPRESENTATIVE

The job of media sales representative requires specialized personal attributes and talents. Sales representatives should be personable, highly articulate, persuasive, and extremely knowledgeable about their media and competitors, particularly as they relate to the needs and sales objectives of advertisers and prospects. What this means is that like a good agency account executive, a top-flight media sales representative should devote a great deal of time and effort to analyzing and understanding the advertiser's business—the problems, opportunities, and competition. The surest way to be an unsuccessful advertising sales representative is to approach an advertiser or agency with a briefcase full of solutions to problems that do not exist for their business. In any field of advertising, it is important to approach each prospect or assignment with as much information and background on the advertiser as is humanly possible. Always be prepared. It will lead to success and save a lot of embarrassment and grief.

OTHER OPPORTUNITIES

In addition to advertising sales opportunities with media firms, there are a number of independent advertising sales rep firms. They offer excellent careers for people who enjoy both sales and advertising. Generally, they specialize in one of the four media areas discussed in this chapter. The larger firms offer on-the-job training and good supervision and guidance. Working for such firms offers diversification, since you usually work on more than one magazine or newspaper or, in the case of broadcast media, on a variety of stations.

Because people working in media sales work so closely with advertisers and advertising agencies, they usually develop good contacts. And since many of the skills needed in the two professions are similar, working in advertising sales can be a valuable first step in an advertising career. Developing skills in advertising sales can lead to a number of positions, including advertising director of a radio station or TV network. In the print field, it may lead to top-level positions, such as publisher of a large magazine. Advertising sales is the basis for most income for the media, and being successful in this area can lead to excellent personal and financial rewards.

CHAPTER

10

PUBLIC RELATIONS, PUBLICITY, SALES PROMOTION, AND DIRECT MAIL

In addition to the jobs available in the country's twelve hundred advertising agencies that are members of the American Association of Advertising Agencies (AAAA) and thousands of small, independent agencies, there are many other employment opportunities in advertising-related fields, including public relations, publicity, sales promotion, and direct mail. A job in any of these areas can provide a lifetime career with opportunity for advancement, security, and creative challenge.

PUBLIC RELATIONS

Public relations and publicity are closely related to advertising. Both fields try to create good and lasting impressions of a product, idea, or service to the public. Some advertising agencies have their own public relations departments, and most corporate marketing and advertising departments oversee corporate public relations. Despite the labels, however, in these situations the people almost always function as publicists. True public relations (PR) is just what the term implies—the art of relating the affairs of an organization and of communicating a favorable impression of that organization to the public. The art of having good public relations was once described as being 95 percent what you do and 5 percent what you say. As a result, public relations counselors and consultants advise clients on their actions as well as on their words. In doing so, they generally deal with the top executives within the companies they serve. Thus, they are required to have a sense of what people outside the organization are thinking and how they are likely to react to the actions of the company.

Public relations professionals need to be mature and have a good perception of what will interest the public. And like advertising professionals, public relations professionals must combine the ability to sell ideas to the media and the public with the skill of communicating effectively in writing. Thus, public relations employees (and publicity employees, too) need a developed promotional flair, advanced writing skills, keen perception of what is newsworthy, and good contacts within the media. In some fields, technical knowledge is also required.

The principal job of many public relations departments is to write day-to-day press releases, ranging from the company president's position on financial performance to the appointment of a new director of human resources. Press releases are created on new products, changes in corporate policy, and corporate issues.

Writing simple press releases is often one of the first jobs given to people starting out in the business. Later, as they acquire more writing and public relations skills, professionals may be asked to write executive speeches or feature articles for publications and reports that represent the organization to shareholders and others.

Other aspects of public relations include placement of press releases and feature stories with the media and arranging for interviews and personal appearances for spokespeople of the company. Just as in advertising, public relations personnel must select appropriate media, whether newspapers, magazines, radio, or television, that will best convey their message to targeted audiences. However, unlike advertising, identifying the media is not enough. Public relations professionals must convince editors, columnists, talk show directors, and others that the story they have is timely, accurate, and of interest to their audience.

Just as advertising account executives must work with clients to convince them of the desirability of their advertisements, the public relations professional must work with clients to convince them how to present material, and at the same time they must work with outside media to convince them to use the material.

PUBLICITY

Publicity and public relations differ from advertising in various ways. Advertising is written and placed exactly as the advertiser designs, since the client pays for it. Publicity, however, and its use and final wording are determined by the editorial staff of the media. In short, the advertiser controls the advertisement, and the media controls publicity.

Publicity involves risks not present in advertising. Publicity provides free exposure for a product or service and may enhance the public image of the product or service.

Moreover, skillfully prepared publicity material appearing as editorial matter adds credibility to the product or service. However, the advertiser or product marketer cannot guarantee that the image will remain positive. The media may completely change a story by the way it is written, rewritten, or reported.

Publicity can take many forms and has many uses. Here is a sampling of the most common activities:

- *New products or services.* In some media, news releases about matters of public interest may be used almost verbatim as submitted. New types of products, announcements of personnel changes, and scheduling of special events are the mainstays of many publications that use press releases with little rewrite. For public relations executives involved in product marketing, the real challenge comes in attracting media coverage for mundane products or routine corporate news.
- *Product demonstrations.* Many new household or personal-care products lend themselves to demonstration on TV daytime talk shows, cable TV food or health channels, and other public interest media. Entertainment publicity, such as the release of a new pop music CD or the announcement of a new big-budget Hollywood film, may find its way onto entertainment news shows such as *Access Hollywood* and *Entertainment Tonight* or the review portions of nightly newscasts.

- *Case histories.* Some products lend themselves to more comprehensive coverage and in-depth case studies. For example, when a health-related discovery changes the public perception of an illness, news and information programmers seek background, examples, and predictions from corporate experts.

- *Newsworthy promotional devices.* Some products are of sufficient interest to a mass audience to make it easy to create a special event. For example, advance fashion news featuring a new collection by a top designer can be made into a major publicity event.

- *Use of prominent personalities.* Some products lend themselves to endorsement by celebrities, experts, or other public figures routinely in the news. Of course, these people expect to be paid for their endorsement, and endorsement fees can cost millions of dollars. National Basketball Association star LeBron James signed to represent shoemaker Nike for $90 million over six years—before he played a single game in the league!

- *Contrived events.* These promotions are usually designed to capture big audiences at sporting events and other activities that draw large crowds. The opportunities are endless, but can include appearance of the Goodyear or Fuji Film blimp at an athletic event or a Hawaiian Tropics beauty contest.

- *Day-to-day activities.* Publicity involves considerable work that is not necessarily glamorous. These day-to-day activities include grinding out releases on the election or promotion of an executive, the opening or closing of a plant, or the appointment of an employee to the chair of some civic or charity organization.

- *Personal publicity.* This sort of work is designed to enhance the reputation of a business client. It may involve ghostwriting speeches, arranging interviews, preparing feature articles, or arranging for the personality to appear as a guest on a television or radio show.

- *Investor relations.* In the twenty-first century, federal regulations on financial disclosure has created a prominent offshoot of public relations known as "investor relations." Investor relations executives specialize in communicating financial results and corporate disclosure required by the Securities and Exchange Commission and other agencies. Investor relations executives need to be financially savvy and trained in compliance requirements. They must also develop a good relationship with senior corporate executives and the security analysts that review their company.

SALES PROMOTION

Sales promotion is yet another advertising-related field that offers great potential. Jobs in sales promotion can be found within advertising agencies, specialized sales promotion companies, and corporate marketing departments.

Sales promotion promotes products and services through the use of sweepstakes, brochures, giveaways, point-of-purchase displays, packaging, direct mail, and even offbeat items such as T-shirts, bumper stickers, and posters. In sales promotion, as in publicity and public relations, there is no commission to be earned by an advertising agency. Income is earned by charges for creative services with fees based on time and often on what the traffic will bear.

In the advertising agency setting, sales promotion may be handled by the client's regular team of account managers, copywriters, art directors, and production people. Sometimes advertising agencies will be hired to do sales promotion for a particular client or project. Sales promotion jobs on the corporate side involve functions similar to those on the agency side—planning, designing, and producing such materials.

Besides the job opportunities available in agencies and corporations, there are a growing number of independent sales promotion firms that offer jobs in this field. For many years, sales promotion has been one of the fastest-growing advertising-related areas, often isolated from the economic pressures of media billing and advertising budgets.

DIRECT MAIL

Direct-mail advertising brings advertising directly into the home and office. It is one of the fastest-growing areas in the field of advertising. Direct mail appears in many sizes, shapes, and forms. At one end of the spectrum is what the public commonly refers to as junk mail, which is impersonal mail simply addressed to "occupant." At the other end of the spectrum are personalized letters addressed to the recipient by name and bearing an authentic signature. Today, telemarketing, or the selling of products and services over the telephone, is helping to expand this field into what is known as direct marketing.

Direct mail may be in the form of letters, postcards, and envelopes with various stuffers, booklets, catalogs, or brochures. Because of computers, people working in direct mail can select names from mailing lists by every possible classification, including zip code, income, type of job, type of previous purchases, amount of purchase, and lifestyle patterns. More and more marketers, both local and national, use direct mail to sell goods and services.

Direct mail is generally more expensive than other major media. The cost to reach a thousand consumers (CPM) is used as a standard measure. Though the return rate of people responding to direct mailing is often as low as a fraction of 1 percent, direct mail is particularly valuable to many advertisers because its response is the most truly measurable of any form of advertising. As a result of continuous testing of offers and different copy and graphics approaches, the responsiveness of different lists can be predicted with surprising accuracy.

Direct mail and direct marketing were once the "poor sisters" of the advertising industry, but no longer. Today, this is a hot field, and many agencies have their own direct-marketing divisions.

Direct mail is a great way to break into the advertising business, especially if you are an aspiring copywriter. Owing to the recent boom in the direct-marketing business, there are many jobs available—many more than in the general advertising areas.

C H A P T E R

11

INTERACTIVE ADVERTISING

In 1993, when computer science students at the University of Illinois at Urbana-Champaign began to noodle around with Mosaic, the first commercial Internet browser that read the graphics and text files created by Hypertext Markup Language (HTML), they may have suspected that they were working on something new and exciting in the world of computer networking. They probably had no idea at all that they were triggering a significant development in marketing, advertising, and mass media.

EVOLUTION OF THE WORLD WIDE WEB AND WEB-BASED ADVERTISING

The Internet itself isn't new. The first computer-based communications network was conceived in the late 1960s by the National Science Foundation and military researchers as a way to accelerate publishing of research information—primarily for military use in the Cold War. It was never meant to be open to the public, and for most of its history—until the mid-1990s—there was nothing on the Internet that anyone would want to read. The network communicated mathematical data mostly and text notes to accompany the research—the first application of what is now a utility for more than 600 million individuals around the world—e-mail.

In 1989, a British physicist working in Switzerland published an essay via the Internet about a concept for revising and expanding the Internet with the new HTML software that allowed computers to not only transmit text and data files but assemble viewable "pages" made of text, graphics, and virtually any other kind of data that could be transmitted. Tim Berners-Lee coined the term *World Wide Web* and the name stuck. Today, the Web is the public face of the global Internet and is hot for more than 1 billion pages of text, graphics, audio, video, and interactive media used by individuals and advertisers.

The advertising industry practically ignored the Web in its early days, noting the relatively small audience (in the tens of thousands at the time) and the complexity of the technology. With no history of media research to support its use and few advertising creative staffers with experience in the technology, there seemed to be no reason to include the concept in client proposals.

Also, in the early 1990s, few agencies had taken the plunge into the computer-based digital graphics technology that supports the Web. Digital scanners that turned photographs into data files were slow and produced poor resolution—far below print advertising standards. Internet connection speeds made looking at Web pages a slow read—fit only for hobbyists and "geeks." Art directors and graphic designers hated HTML because they could never be certain their designs would be read as they were created; the technology restructured pages whenever they were downloaded, changing sizes and fonts to fit an individual user's screen preferences.

But by the late 1990s, it was clear that these geeks were building something special and powerful in the world of mass media. As the connection technology improved, so did the audience base. Web designers developed their own advertising style, banner ads that ran above or below Web page topical content, and markets began to take advantage of the interactive capabilities to create online retail ordering systems.

When a user clicked a computer mouse on the ad, the computer was redirected to the advertiser's own website, where users could make online purchases directly. Some Web designers also stretched the usual boundaries of editorial content and advertising by creating text about products and embedding hot links, or interactive words, in the content that allowed users to click and move directly to a transactional site. Later, the technical pros found ways to sell positions within Internet search engines, the software tools that searched the Web for subjects and key words. Newspapers, in particular, saw the advantages of the technology quickly and began to sell classified ads online, creating a new and efficient personal sales advertising tool. The Web became the ultimate combination of print advertising, point-of-purchase advertising and direct marketing.

In the "dot-com" boom of the late 1990s, computer experts with a bent toward advertising created entrepreneurial interactive advertising agencies—funded with the abundant venture capital. These small agencies sold their services to larger, more traditional agencies, which began to experiment with Web-based interactive advertising. Slowly, these entrepreneurial interactive advertising agencies were acquired by the larger agencies as the venture capital ran out during the dot-com bust of 2001.

Today, most of the larger advertising agencies have Web design departments and interactive advertising specialists in their employ, and interactive advertising is a staple of most campaigns. Print and television advertising almost always includes Internet addresses in text and visuals and refers readers and viewers to websites for more information. Traditional media advertising may even refer its audience to websites for promotional sweepstakes or online ordering.

In 2002, according to the Interactive Advertising Bureau, advertisers spent $6 billion on Internet advertising, down about 16 percent from 2001, a reflection of the recession that began the previous year. Consumer brand advertisers were the largest single advertising group, representing about one-third of all advertising revenue, followed by computer advertisers representing 18 percent of revenue and financial service firms representing 13 percent of revenue.

Banner ads, the mainstay of Internet advertising, accounted for about 29 percent of revenue, followed by classified advertising with 15 percent, hot links with 8 percent, and search engine positions with 4 percent.

JOB OPPORTUNITIES IN INTERACTIVE ADVERTISING

In the early days of World Wide Web advertising, tech pros with little or no formal training in advertising and marketing dominated the industry. Many lacked a college degree, having dropped out to take advantage of the boom. For example, Alex Zoghlin, a University of Illinois student, dropped out in his junior year to start a Web design company, borrowing $50,000 from his father, a financial consultant. Five years later, he sold Neoglyphics, a pioneer in Web-based advertising, for $60 million and moved on to help found Orbitz, a travel industry website owned by the leading airlines.

After the 2001 recession, however, the interactive ad business became more formal and the job requirements more demanding. Computer technicians may be able to get by with a two-year technical degree and software training, but senior executives need a business or marketing degree or specialized training in "E-commerce" to get the top jobs with the leading agencies.

Here are some of the key jobs in interactive advertising.

Producer

Like a television spot producer, the interactive producer has broad responsibility for creating interactive advertising. Working with the account services staff and the agency creative directors, the producer determines the nature of interactive advertising—banner ads, search engine positions, hot links—and how to thematically match interactive advertising with ads created for other media. The producer may work with copy written for print ads, graphics created for print ads, audio for radio and TV ads, and video for broadcast, melding them all into website use.

The entry-level employee, a production assistant, may assemble and help choose audio, video, and graphic components and help edit ad copy for use on websites. The production assistant may also need to use digital graphics tools such as scanners and digital cameras to capture images for websites and digital recorders for audio. The job doesn't require a college degree to start, but an undergraduate degree will help an assistant get promoted more swiftly in large agencies.

Job requirements include extensive training in basic computer software, familiarity with HTML and software editors such as Dreamweaver, and a strong understanding of the interactive and transactive capabilities of the Web. A producer or production assistant also needs to work well with other agency departments and meet group goals and objectives.

Web Designer

A Web designer takes the concepts developed by a producer and turns them into a series of Web pages or Web ads—manipulating the real estate of a computer screen into a visual and interactive design. Web designers treat their audience as "users," not just readers or viewers as in other media. They must direct advertising users to perform tasks online, such as click on a banner ad or hot link or make an ordering choice.

A Web designer may be hired directly from a college program in computer graphics, E-commerce, or Web design or may be hired based on a portfolio of Web pages and turned loose on big accounts, because familiarity with the latest technology leads to the coolest and most interactive pages. But successful Web designers also need a basic understanding of business goals and general advertising concepts. An in-depth understanding of HTML and its successor, Extensible Markup Language (XML), and of digital editing and graphics tools is essential.

Programmer

The equivalent of a staff artist in the art department, the programmer creates the computer code that is assembled as a Web advertisement, including the text, graphics, audio, and video components as well as database applications that drive such features as online polls, ordering, and the personalization of Web pages, such as Amazon's "your store" function.

Entry-level programmers need professional-level abilities in computer programming for the Web, including "scratch" coding of HTML, database applications, and other functions. Self-training used to be enough in the early days of interactive advertising, but now a two-year technical degree is essential, with a four-year degree preferred.

CHAPTER

12

GETTING
A JOB AND
MOVING
AHEAD

The advertising job market should resume growth now that we seem to be emerging from the recession of the early 2000s. It is an industry that offers opportunity for those who have a creative mind and the willingness to work.

CAREER INFORMATION

A good place to start collecting information is from the people closest to you—your family and friends. These personal contacts are often overlooked, but they can be extremely helpful. These people may be able to answer your questions directly or, just as important, put you in touch with someone who can. This "networking" can lead to an "informational interview," where you can meet with someone who is willing to answer your questions about a career or a particular company and who can provide inside information on related fields and other helpful hints. This is a highly effective way to learn the recommended type of training for certain positions, how someone in that position entered and advanced, and what he or she likes and dislikes about the work. While developing your network of contacts, you may want to begin exploring other avenues.

Public libraries, career centers, and guidance offices have a great deal of career material. To begin your library search, look in the card catalog or at the computer listings under "Vocations" or "Careers" and then under specific fields. Also, leaf through the file of pamphlets that describe employment in different organizations. Check the periodicals section, where you will find trade and professional magazines and journals about specific occupations and industries. Familiarize yourself with the concerns and activities of potential employers by skimming their annual reports and other information they distribute to the public.

The Internet is also a great resource for job hunters. Many professions, including the advertising field, now post open jobs in various online job databases, the largest of which is Monster.com (monster.com). America's Job Bank (ajb.com) and CareerBuilder (careerbuilder.com) is also recommended. Always assess career guidance materials carefully. Information should be current. Beware of materials produced by schools for recruitment purposes that seem to glamorize the occupation, overstate the earnings, or exaggerate the demand for workers.

You may wish to seek help from a counselor. Counselors are trained to help you discover your strengths and weaknesses, guide you through an evaluation of your goals and values, and help you determine what you want in a career.

The counselor will not tell you what to do, but will administer interest inventories and aptitude tests, interpret the results, and help you explore your options. Counselors also may be able to discuss local job markets and the entry requirements and costs of the schools, colleges, or training programs offering preparation for the kind of work that interests you. You can find counselors in

- High school guidance offices
- College career planning and placement offices
- Placement offices in private vocational/technical schools and institutions
- Vocational rehabilitation agencies
- Counseling services offered by community organizations
- Private counseling agencies and private practices
- State employment service offices affiliated with the U.S. Employment Service

Professional societies, trade associations, labor unions, business firms, and educational institutions provide a variety of free or inexpensive career material. For information on occupations not covered here, consult directories in your library's reference section for the names of potential sources. You may need to start with *The Guide to American Directories* or *The Directory of Directories*. Another useful resource is *The Encyclopedia of Associations*, an annual multivolume publication listing trade associations, professional societies, labor unions, and fraternal and patriotic organizations.

For firsthand experience in an occupation, you may wish to intern or take a summer or part-time job. Some internships offer academic credit or pay a stipend. Check with guidance offices, college career resource centers, or directly with employers.

For help in locating state or local area information, contact your state occupational information coordinating committee (SOICC). These committees may provide the information directly or refer you to other sources.

Most states have a career information delivery system (CIDS). Look for this system in secondary schools, postsecondary institutions, libraries, job-training sites, vocational rehabilitation centers, and employment service offices. Job seekers can use the system's computers, printed material, microfiche, and toll-free hotlines to obtain information on occupations, educational opportunities, student financial aid, apprenticeships, and military careers. Ask counselors and the SOICC for specific locations.

State employment security agencies develop detailed information about local labor markets, such as current and projected employment by occupation and industry, characteristics of the workforce, and changes in state and local area economic activity.

EDUCATION AND TRAINING

Almost all colleges, schools, and training institutes readily reply to any requests for information. When contacting these institutions, you may want to inquire about

- Admission requirements
- Courses offered
- Certificates or degrees awarded
- Cost
- Available financial aid
- Location and size of school

Check with professional and trade associations for lists of schools that offer career preparation in a field you're interested in. Guidance offices and libraries usually have the kinds of directories discussed shortly as well as college catalogs, which can provide more information on specific institutions. Be sure to use the latest edition because many directories and catalogs are revised annually.

Financial Aid

Information about financial aid is available from a variety of sources. Contact your high school guidance counselor and college financial aid officer for information concerning scholarships, fellowships, grants, loans, and work-study programs. In addition, every state administers financial aid programs; contact state departments of education for information. Banks and credit unions can provide information about student loans. You also may want to consult the directories and guides to sources of student financial aid available in guidance offices and public libraries.

The federal government provides grants, loans, work-study programs, and other benefits to students. Information about programs administered by the U.S. Department of Education is presented in *The Student Aid Guide,* updated annually. To get a copy, write to the Federal Student Aid Information Center, c/o Federal Student Aid Programs, P.O. Box 84, Washington, DC 20044, or phone, toll-free, 1-800-USA-LEARN.

Meeting College Costs, an annual publication of the College Board, explains how student financial aid works and how to apply for it. The current edition is available to high school students through guidance counselors.

Some student aid programs are designed to assist specific groups—Hispanics, African Americans, Native Americans, or women, for example. *Higher Education Opportunities for Minorities and Women,* published by the U.S. Department of Education (ed.gov), is a guide to organizations offering assistance. This publication can be found in libraries and guidance offices, and copies may be obtained from the U.S. Department of Education, 400 Maryland Avenue, SW, Washington, DC 20202 (phone: 1-800-USA-LEARN).

The armed forces have several educational assistance programs. These include the Reserve Officers' Training Corps (ROTC), the New GI bill, and tuition assistance. Information can be obtained from military recruiting centers, located in most cities.

It takes some people a great deal of time and effort to find a job they enjoy. Others may walk right into an ideal employment situation. Don't be discouraged if you have to pursue many leads. Friends, neighbors, teachers, and counselors may know of available jobs in your field of interest. Read the want ads. Consult state employment service offices and private or nonprofit employment agencies, or contact employers directly.

Informal Job Search Methods

It is possible to apply directly to employers without a referral. You may locate a potential employer in the Yellow Pages, in directories of local chambers of commerce, and in other directories that provide information about employers. When you find an employer you are interested in, you can file an application even if you don't know for certain that an opening exists.

Want Ads

The help-wanted ads in newspapers identify hundreds of jobs. Realize, however, that many job openings are *not* listed there. Also, be aware that the classified ads sometimes do not give important information. Many offer little or no description of the job, working conditions, or pay. Some ads do not identify the employer. They may simply give a post office box for sending your résumé. This makes follow-up difficult. Furthermore, some ads are for out-of-town jobs, and others advertise employment agencies rather than employment.

Keep the following in mind if you are using want ads:

- Do not rely solely on the classifieds to find a job; follow other leads as well.
- Answer ads promptly, since openings may be filled quickly, even before the ad stops appearing in the paper.
- Follow the ads diligently. Check them every day, as early as possible, to give yourself an advantage.
- Beware of "no experience necessary" ads. These ads often signal low wages, poor working conditions, or straight commission work.

- Keep a record of all ads to which you have responded, including the specific skills, educational background, and personal qualifications required for the position.

Public Employment Service

The state employment service, sometimes called the Job Service, operates in coordination with the Labor Department's U.S. Employment Service. About seventeen hundred local offices, also known as employment service centers, help job seekers locate employment and help employers find qualified workers at no cost to themselves. To find the office nearest you, look in the state government telephone listings under "Job Service" or "Employment."

A computerized job network system—America's Job Bank—run by the U.S. Department of Labor, lists thousands of jobs each week. Job seekers can access these listings through the use of a personal computer in any local public employment service office, as well as in several hundred military installations. In addition, some state employment agencies have set up America's Job Bank in other settings, including libraries, schools, shopping malls, and correctional facilities. A wide range of jobs are listed.

Tips for Finding the Right Job, a U.S. Department of Labor pamphlet, offers advice on determining your job skills, organizing your job search, writing a résumé, and making the most of an interview. *Job Search Guide: Strategies for Professionals*, another U.S. Department of Labor publication, also discusses specific steps that job seekers can follow to identify employment opportunities. This publication includes sections on handling your job loss, managing your personal resources, assessing your skills and interests, researching the job market, conducting the job search and networking, writing résumés and cover letters, employment interviewing and testing, and sources of additional information. Check with your state employment service office, or order a copy of these publications from the U.S. Government Printing Office.

Job Matching and Referral

At a state employment service office, an interviewer will determine if you are "job ready" or if counseling and testing services would be helpful before you begin your job search. These centers can test for occupational aptitudes and interests and then help you choose and prepare for a career.

After you are "job ready," you may examine America's Job Bank, a computerized listing of public- and private-sector job openings that is updated daily. Select openings that interest you, then get more details from a staff member, who can describe the job openings in detail and arrange for interviews with prospective employers.

Services for Special Groups

By law, veterans are entitled to priority at state employment service centers. Veterans' employment representatives can inform you of available assistance and help you deal with any problems.

Summer Youth Programs provide summer jobs in city, county, and state government agencies for low-income youth. Students, school dropouts, or graduates entering the labor market who are between sixteen and twenty-one years of age are eligible. In addition, the Job Corps, with more than a hundred centers throughout the United States, helps young people learn skills or obtain education.

Service centers also refer applicants to opportunities available under the Job Training Partnership Act (JTPA) of 1982. JTPA prepares economically disadvantaged persons and those facing barriers to employment.

Private Employment Agencies

Private employment agencies can be very helpful, but don't forget that they are in business to make money. Most agencies operate on a commission basis, with the fee dependent on a successful match. You or the hiring company will have to pay a fee for the service. Find out the exact cost and who is responsible for paying it before using the service.

While employment agencies can help you save time and contact employers who otherwise may be difficult to locate, the costs may sometimes outweigh the benefits. Consider any guarantee they offer when figuring the cost.

College Career Planning and Placement Offices

College placement offices help match job openings with suitable job seekers. You can schedule appointments and use available facilities for interviews with recruiters, or you can scan the lists of part-time, temporary, and summer jobs maintained in many of these offices. You also can get counseling, testing, and job search advice and take advantage of their career resource library. Here you will also be able to identify and evaluate your interests, work values, and skills; attend workshops on such topics as job search strategy, résumé writing, letter writing, and effective interviewing; critique drafts of résumés and videotapes of mock interviews; explore files of résumés and references; and attend job fairs conducted by the office.

Community Agencies

Many nonprofit organizations offer counseling, career development, and job placement services, generally targeted to a particular group, such as women, youth, minorities, ex-offenders, or older workers. Many cities have commissions that provide services for these special groups.

Many communities have career counseling, training, placement, and support services for employment. These programs are sponsored by a variety of organizations, including churches and synagogues, nonprofit organizations, social service agencies, the state employment service, and vocational rehabilitation agencies.

WHERE THE JOBS ARE

In Chapter 8, we discussed the rapidly increasing job opportunities in corporate advertising. However, it is within the advertising agencies that most entry-level advertising staff are employed. There are many agencies across the country and throughout the world, from huge conglomerates to smaller boutique agencies, all competing for a finite amount of advertising spending. Whether you would feel more comfortable at a large agency or small agency, opportunities exist, but you must be clever to land the job of your choice.

You can find information on the top fifty agencies based in the United States by gross income in a publication called the *Fact Pack*, published every year by *Advertising Age*; this document is also available for use online at AdAge.com. Inside the *Fact Pack* is a listing of the largest agencies in this country, and many of them employ several thousand employees. Use this chart as a guide when looking for employment at a larger agency. Success breeds success, and many of these firms need fresh, new ideas and new people at this very moment.

The most successful agencies feel the pressure to continue to grow and expand. While in a growth mode, agencies offer greater job opportunities and chances for advancement. But it also holds true that with a loss of major accounts or during a depressed economy, they can slide down quickly.

Megagroups

A megagroup is an advertising conglomerate that also deals in nonmedia advertising and related areas, such as consulting, public relations, and direct response. Megagroups are typically worldwide operations that started as advertising agencies and branched out into other service areas as their advertising business became more and more successful. It is possible to become employed at a large agency or megagroup in a nonagency type of job, owing to the wide range of positions offered by these companies.

The megagroups tend to be divided into two main branches: communications and consulting. The areas associated with advertising agencies in general, such as advertising, public relations, and sales promotion, are found in the communications branch. Those areas not normally found in advertising agencies, such as marketing and sales, litigation services, and technology development, fall under consulting. In larger operations, a greater variety of possible employment opportunities are available. Opportunities for attorneys and personnel managers interested in working in an advertising agency environment can be found within many of these megagroups.

GETTING STARTED

Before applying for your first job, you need to decide what you want to do or be in advertising—the kind of job that would be most beneficial for both you and your employer. Note the concern for how the employer will benefit. Never forget that the job hunter must always focus on what he or she has to offer the prospective employer. In simple terms, the question to be addressed is "What can I do for you?" not "What can you do for me?"

In deciding what type of advertising job suits you best, try to analyze your strengths and weaknesses. What do you do well? What kind of useful and applicable experience have you had? What sort of things do you like to do, and why? What do you dislike doing, and why? Are you impatient with details? Are you inclined to be analytical? Are you at ease with people, or do you prefer to stay in the background?

This kind of self-analysis is useful and not nearly as difficult as it sounds. But it does take deliberate thought and a totally honest appraisal of yourself. When you have completed your self-analysis, you will be in a position to zero in on the kind of job for which you are best qualified and at which you are most likely to succeed. You may also find that you have weaknesses that you need to overcome. It is not a bad idea to check your findings with someone whom you respect and trust to verify your conclusions. You must take into account how your own strengths and weaknesses relate to the advertising field. Consider the types of employment available within an agency or corporate department and decide where, if anywhere, you will fit. Success in advertising takes a particular type of personality and temperament. Make sure that you possess the personal characteristics necessary for success in this field.

Next, find out where you are likely to find the kind of job you want. Then make your plans to cover that territory. If you want to work for a big agency, concentrate on the major advertising centers like New York City, Chicago, Detroit, Dallas, Boston, San Francisco, Minneapolis, and Los Angeles. If you think a smaller agency might be your first choice, you can look in these same cities as well as smaller cities and perhaps even your own hometown.

The *Standard Directory of Advertising Agencies* will give you the locations and sizes of different firms. You should be able to find a copy at your local library, or try to borrow one from a friend in advertising. Reading trade publications such as *Advertising Age* to look at the help-wanted ads and see which agencies landed new accounts may provide you with direction as to which agencies are looking for new employees.

RÉSUMÉS

After you have pinpointed the type of job you want and where you would like to work, you must prepare a résumé outlining your qualifications. Most people approach this task with considerable apprehension, no matter how far along they are in their career. The challenge of writing a résumé is to say enough to arouse interest and convey assurance that you are truly a qualified applicant without overstating your accomplishments and abilities in a way that is likely to turn off your potential employer. Remember, advertising is communication and selling. Here is your chance to show how well you can sell yourself. It will help if you follow these basic rules:

1. Be concise.
2. List relevant employment activities in reverse order (the most recent one first). Be sure to include part-time jobs you have had, especially those in sales or media that might be pertinent to advertising. Often these job experiences are more important than your academic achievements.
3. Try not to overstate or understate achievements. If you are modest, do not forget that the person looking at your résumé can only make a judgment on the basis of what is written. If you are inclined to be a little exuberant, remember that exaggerated claims are sure to reduce your credibility. Be as objective as possible.
4. Include academic achievements and especially extracurricular activities that show a flair for creativity and promotion. Perhaps you were chairperson for the fraternity or sorority formal or handled publicity for the school football team. These are important activities and should be mentioned. Be sure to include any evidence of leadership qualities (class officer, team captain), as these qualities are always in demand.
5. Record information about pertinent hobbies or leisure-time activities, like painting, photography, short-story writing, or music composition. These things are closely related to the work in advertising.
6. Do not forget to include your address, e-mail address, and telephone number.
7. Give references. Provide name, title, and address for three or four people whose judgments and opinions about you are likely to carry some weight. If they happen to be advertising executives, so much the better.
8. Prepare your résumé on standard 8½ × 11 inch white bond paper. It is easiest for people to handle. Also, save a digital version of your résumé as a text or Rich Text Format file for transmission to a prospective employer.

It is a good idea to write a cover letter to accompany your résumé setting forth the job you want and adding a few details as to why you believe you are qualified. Do not, however, discuss salary. Such discussions come after you and your future employer have agreed that there is a mutually acceptable opening for you.

If you have letters of recommendation (or commendation), attach copies to your résumé or make them part of your portfolio. The more evidence you have of your employability, the better.

Never hesitate to ask personal and family friends or former employers to provide you with an introduction to anyone who might have a job for you. They probably will be happy to assist you, and the contact they provide will help you broaden your network of associations in the business.

Here are a few reminders to help you compose a well-constructed résumé:

- State your name, address, telephone number, and e-mail address.
- State your employment objective. State the type of work or specific job you are seeking.
- State your education, including school name and address, dates of attendance, curriculum, and highest grade completed or degree awarded.
- Describe your experience, paid or volunteer. Include the following for each job: job title, name and address of employer, dates of employment, and job duties.
- Describe any special skills, knowledge of machinery, proficiency in foreign languages, honors or awards received, and membership in organizations.
- Note on your résumé that "references are available upon request." On a separate sheet, list three or four references, giving name, address, telephone number, and job title for each.

PORTFOLIOS

In addition to a résumé, you should also prepare a portfolio of your best advertising work before you schedule your interviews. As an entry-level job seeker, you probably face the problem of not having many published samples of your work. Do, however, include articles you have written for the student newspaper and relevant projects you prepared for class. But do not include any sample unless you feel it represents your best work. If you don't have many samples, create some. Serious candidates without a college degree in marketing or advertising can enhance their job portfolio with preparation at the advertising industry–supported Portfolio Center in Atlanta, Georgia. The center offers a two-year program of studies in advertising and graphic design for job candidates in the field.

The quality most likely to attract an employer is your creativity. How good are you at coming up with original, sparkling ideas? In creating ads for your portfolio, you need to demonstrate this quality. Study familiar products, and try to come up with a novel way to sell them. Do some research on the product to determine its current uses and possible unknown uses. Study what benefits the product has for you and other consumers. Just as you would for a real advertising campaign, base your ad on what you learn.

What you include in your ad also depends on what type of job you are seeking. If you want a position as an artist, the design of the ad should be of primary importance. This does not mean that you need to do a finished ad—just enough to show your capabilities. And don't fail to include at least a headline for your ad. If you see yourself mainly as a writer, the design for the ad does not have to be detailed, although clearly indicate the illustration area within the ad. Concentrate on writing a striking headline (or more than one) as well as at least part of the body copy, the explanatory copy for the ad. And in either case, if you have any knowledge or experience in television production, scripts and storyboards showing the major frames in your ad can also be included in your portfolio.

INTERVIEWS

Once you have prepared your résumé and portfolio, you are ready for your first interview. Try to arrange an appointment with the agency's creative director or copy chief or the head of any department that interests you. Human resources directors are less likely to be interested in or impressed with your work than department heads. When the time for the interview arrives, be punctual. Remember, good manners and proper dress are recognized quickly, and first impressions are important, especially in a business like advertising, where one's image is important.

Interviews can be nerve-racking experiences because you will probably be expected to do most of the talking. The line between "running off at the mouth" and not saying enough can be very thin, particularly if you encounter an interviewer who stares at you in silence. Consequently, you should consider what you want to communicate and carefully organize what you are going to say. Your emphasis should be on why you want a job with this company (not why you want a job; the interviewer knows that) and why you believe you are qualified for the position.

Go to the interview prepared with intelligent questions about the kind of work available and the contribution you can make. Do research about the prospective employer before the interview. Listen to the answers and try to create a dialogue. Ask questions that encourage the interviewer to talk with you. The interviewer will like you better if you can get him or her to do some of the talking.

Whatever you do, do not focus your questions on such things as vacation policies, employee benefits, or anything else that suggests that you are more interested in what the company can do for you than in what you can do for the company. The employer will provide this information, usually near the end of the interview. If it is not offered, the appropriate time to discuss it is after the employer has had an opportunity to bring up the subject. Before leaving, determine when you might learn the outcome of your interview. Ask if you may phone back in two or three days. Make an effort to keep the door open for future contact. If employment seems unlikely, ask the interviewer if he or she knows of an opportunity at another company. You may pick up a good lead that will help you land your first job.

Unfortunately, few job applicants are hired at the first place they visit, and trying to get on someone's payroll is often time consuming and discouraging. For those reasons, do not let your initial hopes run too high or your early disappointments run too deep. Getting the right job, like most other worthwhile achievements in life, requires a systematic approach, hard work, determination, and persistence.

Here are a few additional interviewing tips:

Preparation

- Learn about the organization.
- Have a specific job (or jobs) in mind.
- Review your qualifications for the job.
- Prepare answers to broad questions about yourself.
- Review your résumé.

- Practice an interview with a friend or relative.
- Arrive before the scheduled time of your interview.

Personal Appearance
- Be well groomed.
- Dress appropriately.
- Do not chew gum or smoke.

The Interview
- Answer each question concisely.
- Respond promptly.
- Use good manners. Learn the name of your interviewer and shake hands as you meet.
- Use proper English and avoid slang.
- Be cooperative and enthusiastic.
- Ask questions about the position and the organization.
- Thank the interviewer, and follow up with a letter.

Test (If Employer Gives One)
- Listen closely to instructions.
- Read each question carefully.
- Write legibly and clearly.
- Budget your time wisely, and don't dwell on one question.

Information to Bring to an Interview
- Social Security number.
- Driver's license number.
- Résumé. Although not all employers require applicants to bring a résumé, you should be able to furnish the interviewer with information about your education, training, and previous employment.
- Most employers require three references. Get permission from people before using their names, and make sure they will give you a good reference. Try to avoid using relatives. For each reference, provide the following information: name, address, telephone number, and job title.

MAKING YOUR DECISION

Does it make any difference to you whether the company is private or public? A private company may be controlled by an individual or a family, which can mean that key jobs are reserved for relatives and friends. A public company is controlled by a board of directors responsible to the stockholders. Key jobs are open to anyone with talent.

Is the organization in an industry with favorable long-term prospects? The most successful firms tend to be in industries that are growing rapidly.

Where is the job located? If it is in another city, you need to consider the cost of living, the availability of housing and transportation, and the quality of educational and recreational facilities in the new location. Even if the place of work is in your area, consider the time and expense of commuting and whether it can be done by public transportation.

Where are the firm's headquarters and branches located? Although a move may not be required now, future opportunities could depend on your willingness to move to these places.

It is often easy to get background information on an organization simply by telephoning its public relations office. A public company's annual report to the stockholders tells about its corporate philosophy, history, products or services, goals, and financial status. Most government agencies can furnish reports that describe their programs and missions. Press releases, company newsletters or magazines, and recruitment brochures also can be useful. Ask the organization for any other items that might interest a prospective employee.

Background information on the organization also may be available at your public or school library. If you cannot get an annual report, check the library for reference directories that provide basic facts about the company, such as earnings, products and services, and number of employees. Here are some directories widely available in libraries: *Dun and Bradstreet's Million Dollar Directory; Standard and Poor's Register of Corporations, Directors and Executives; Moody's Industrial Manual; Thomas' Register of American Manufacturers;* and *Ward's Business Directory.* If you plan to continue your job search, these directories will also list the names and addresses of other firms that might hire you.

Stories about an organization in magazines and newspapers can tell a great deal about its successes, failures, and plans for the future. You can find articles about a company by looking under its name in periodical or computerized indexes, such as the *Business Periodicals Index, Reader's Guide to Periodical Literature, Newspaper Index, Wall Street Journal Index,* and *New York Times Index.* It probably will not be useful to look back more than two or three years.

The library also may have government publications that present projections of growth for the industry in which the organization is classified. Long-term projections of employment and output for more than two hundred industries, covering the entire economy, are developed by the Bureau of Labor Statistics and revised every other year; see the November 1995 *Monthly Labor Review* for the most recent projections. The *U.S. Industrial Outlook,* published annually by the U.S. Department of Commerce, presents detailed analysis of growth prospects for many industries. Trade magazines also have frequent articles on the trends for specific industries.

Career centers at colleges and universities often have information on employers that is not available in libraries. Ask the career center librarian how to find out about a particular organization. The career center may have an entire file of information on the company.

The Nature of the Work

Even if everything else about the job is good, you will be unhappy if you dislike the day-to-day work. Determining in advance whether you will like the work may be difficult. However, the more you find out about it before accepting or rejecting the job offer, the more likely you are to make the right choice. Ask yourself questions like the following:

- Does the work match your interests and make good use of your skills? The duties and responsibilities of the job should be explained in enough detail to answer this question.
- How important is the job in this company? An explanation of where you fit in the organization and how you are supposed to contribute to its overall objectives should give an idea of the job's importance.
- Are you comfortable with the supervisor?
- Do the other employees seem friendly and cooperative?
- Does the work require travel?

- Does the job call for irregular hours?
- How long do most people who enter this job stay with the company? High turnover can mean dissatisfaction with the nature of the work or with something else about the job.

Opportunities for Promotion

A good job offers you opportunities to grow and move up. It gives you a chance to learn new skills, increase your earnings, and rise to positions of greater authority, responsibility, and prestige. A lack of opportunities can dampen interest in the work and result in frustration and boredom.

The company should have a training plan. You know what your abilities are now. What valuable new skills does the company plan to teach you?

The employer should give you some idea of promotion possibilities within the organization. What is the next step on the career ladder? If you have to wait for a job to become vacant before you can be promoted, how long does this usually take? Employers differ on their policies regarding promotion from within the organization. When opportunities for advancement do arise, will you compete with applicants from outside the company? Can you apply for jobs for which you qualify elsewhere within the organization, or is mobility within the firm limited?

Salary and Benefits

Wait for the employer to introduce these subjects. Most companies will not talk about pay until they have decided to hire you. To know if their offer is reasonable, you need a rough estimate of what the job should pay. You may have to go to several sources for this information. Talk to friends who recently were hired in similar jobs. Ask your teachers and the staff in the college placement office about starting pay for graduates with your qualifications. Scan the help-wanted ads in newspapers. Check the library or your school's career center for salary surveys, such as the *College Placement Council Salary Survey* and Bureau of Labor Statistics occupational wage surveys. If you are considering the salary and benefits for a job in another geographic area, make allowances for differences in the cost of living, which may be significantly higher in a large metropolitan area than in a smaller city, town, or rural area. Use the research to come up with a base salary range for yourself, the top being the best you can hope to get and the bottom being the least you will take. An employer cannot be specific about the amount of pay if it includes commissions and bonuses. The way the plan works, however, should be explained. The employer also should be able to tell you what most people in the job earn.

You should also learn the organization's policy regarding overtime. Depending on the job, you may or may not be exempt from laws requiring the employer to compensate you for overtime. Find out how many hours you will be expected to work each week and whether you receive overtime pay or compensatory time off for working more than the specified number of hours in a week.

Also take into account that the starting salary is just that, the start. Your salary should be reviewed on a regular basis—many organizations do it every twelve months. If the employer is pleased with your performance, how much can you expect to earn after one, two, or three or more years?

Don't think of your salary as the only compensation you will receive. Consider benefits. Benefits can add a lot to your base pay. Health insurance and pension plans are among the most important benefits. Other common benefits include life insurance, paid vacations and holidays, and sick leave. Benefits vary widely between smaller and larger firms, between full-time and part-time workers, and between the public and private sectors. Find out exactly what the benefit package includes and how much of the costs you must bear.

When you evaluate a job offer, you have many things to consider. Only you will be able to weigh the advantages of a job that is more compatible with your interests and skills against a job that offers higher salary and more promising advancement opportunities, or weigh the advantages of a job that offers better benefits against a job that is much closer to your home.

Asking yourself these kinds of questions won't guarantee that you make the best career decision—only hindsight can do that—but you probably will make a better choice than if you act on impulse.

Detailed data on wages and benefits are available from the Bureau of Labor Statistics, (bls.gov), 2 Massachusetts Avenue, NE, Room 4160, Washington, DC 20212-0001 (phone: (202) 691-6199). Data on weekly earnings, based on the *Current Population Survey*, is available from the Bureau of Labor Statistics, Office of Employment and Unemployment Statistics, 2 Massachusetts Avenue, NE, Room 4945, Washington, DC 20212.

ON-THE-JOB TRAINING

It used to be customary for a beginner to start in either print production or traffic. Some agencies still start newcomers in these departments, but the length of time they stay there is usually brief.

Today, it is more common to place beginners in other departments, such as media or research, or in a training program that systematically moves them from place to place. In this manner, it is certain they will have an opportunity to become familiar with the various agency activities before being given definitive job assignments. Training programs differ from agency to agency in the sequence of departments that are observed, the length of time devoted to each, and the amount of actual participation as opposed to observation.

Bearing in mind that these differences do exist, a typical course of instruction might include the following:

Traffic and Print Production
- Agency procedures
- Assignments
- Relationship with other departments
- Printing processes, tours of printing and engraving plants and typesetting shops
- Planning and buying print material other than advertisements—booklets, brochures, posters, displays
- Legal requirements
- Security regulations and procedures
- Correspondence, mailing, and shipping

Research Department
- Gathering and analyzing market information
- Developing a marketing or advertising strategy
- Designing market research procedures and questionnaires
- Using and reporting results
- Using copy research in its various forms for print and broadcast
- Identifying and evaluating competitive media research
- Measuring the reach (number of people who see or hear the advertising) and frequency (how often they see or hear it) of various media choices and selecting from various media alternatives

Media Services Department

- Fitting the media plan and strategy to marketing and advertising goals
- Evaluating and contracting for network programs and spots
- Evaluating and buying market-by-market programs and spots
- Evaluating and selecting magazines and newspapers that best fit each advertising plan.

Creative Services Department

- Understanding how advertising is designed to fit the specifications of the plan and what thinking and discussion go into developing the plan
- Learning how illustrative material is chosen and sources from which it may be obtained
- Understanding how a TV commercial takes its form from rough idea to storyboard to finished product, including visits to film studios, animation studios, and on-location filming
- Learning how a radio commercial comes into being and different techniques available, and visiting recording studios
- Casting and talent selection
- Codes and rules of the involved guilds
- Legal and regulatory restrictions and guidelines
- Budget control

Account Services Department

- Duties and assignments
- Formulating a marketing strategy
- Fitting the advertising plan to marketing strategy
- Reporting results of client meetings, including assignments for action
- Dealing with agency personnel in other departments
- Managing the client's advertising budget
- Directing agency activities for a profit
- Legal and regulatory consideration

If the agency is engaged in promotional or merchandising activities, there may also be some instruction in these areas. It would probably include these topics:

- Special requirements of sales promotion copy
- Sales promotion art and design
- Organizing sales meetings, including presentation techniques
- Using premiums, giveaways, and contests and selecting suppliers
- Finding and taking advantage of publicity opportunities
- Legal and regulatory requirements (important because each state has different rules with respect to contests and premium offers)
- Managing the budget

There are different theories about how best to train beginners and help them learn all the facets of the job. The important thing to remember, however, is that whatever procedure is used, it will be only as effective and valuable as each trainee's interest and application permit it to be. If the desire to learn the advertising business is strong, it really does not matter how the training program is designed. In addition, it should be remembered that such programs are only the beginning. For the true advertising professional, the learning process never stops.

Large mass-marketers of consumer goods (particularly in the food field), such as Procter and Gamble, General Mills, and Kellogg, offer excellent training programs in advertising. There is a definite advantage to such programs in that one learns of the movement of goods from the client's point of view. This experience, gained early on, can be useful in later work in an advertising agency. By training within the corporate advertising department, one can learn about the effects of an advertising campaign on the sales and profitability of goods over a period of time. Of course, this experience does not have to lead to agency work; there are plenty of lifetime opportunities in advertising in the corporate setting.

PROMOTION AND ADVANCEMENT

After working on the job for a while, you will no doubt start thinking about promotion and advancement. Here, again, it is impossible to set down any definite guidelines. Advertising is not like government employment, in which so many years at one job level entitle an employee to move up to the next higher spot. How fast you progress in advertising depends almost entirely on your performance, your ability to acquire the necessary skills, your maturity, your grasp of the business, and the success of your employer, whether it is an advertising agency or a corporate marketer. It is impossible to make an absolute statement about how quickly and to what level a new employee will advance in the advertising business. However, here are some general observations that apply to most beginners.

Do not expect to begin your advancement immediately. If you are hired right out of college as a trainee, it will probably be a year or two before you find yourself working full-time at some specialty—account work, media research, creative work, or whatever. From that point on, your progress can be rapid if you are capable and if there aren't a number of equally competent people ahead of you.

Assuming that you have a clear track to an open position, that the agency you are working for is successful and growing, and that you have the necessary ability, you are poised for success. In that case, it would be natural for your steps up the ladder to proceed at a fairly fast pace, possibly as follows:

- One and a half years training in media
- Two years as an assistant account executive
- Five years as an account executive and senior account executive
- Two to three years as an account manager, becoming a vice president
- Three to five years as a management supervisor, possibly becoming an executive vice president, depending on the agency's structure
- Agency president

At some point during your advancement, you will become a member of the agency's board of directors and perhaps a stockholder. And as you progress, you will have opportunities to acquire increasing amounts of stock in the agency. Exactly the same kind of progression takes place on the creative side of the business. It can also happen in media or research.

It used to be a rarity for a large and prestigious agency to have a president (or chief executive officer) that was not well into his or her forties; however, this is no longer the case, especially in advertising. So if you are especially dynamic and talented, you can make it to the top in a relatively short period of time.

If you are member of a minority group and have the necessary talent, advertising offers real opportunities for you. Every sizable company or agency is eager to add people of different ethnic backgrounds to its staff. In most advertising centers, minorities are in great demand and also in short supply. With more and more specialized print media, and with more and more choices for channels on television, we are going to see media targeted toward minorities. The move in television is toward "narrowcasting" as opposed to "broadcasting." The Spanish-speaking population is, of course, at the head of the list. There are approximately 30 million native Spanish-speaking people now living in the United States. And as a growing number of agencies recognize the potential of marketing to ethnic groups as special markets, these opportunities will increase.

There are also African American and Hispanic advertising agencies, generally concentrated in major urban areas. They usually specialize in advertising to the African American or Spanish-speaking markets and solicit clients to reach these sectors only. These agencies have grown tremendously in the last twenty years and offer many opportunities.

FREELANCING OR STARTING YOUR OWN AGENCY

Nearly everyone gets started in advertising working for someone else, whether that someone is an advertising agency, a corporate advertising department, or a firm specializing in some aspect of advertising. Before you consider freelancing—that is, selling your creative or marketing skills as an individual to various advertisers and advertising agencies—or starting an agency of your own, you need to gain experience and enough skill to make yourself marketable to prospective clients.

Freelancing provides a good first step in self-employment, especially for people in the creative side of advertising. As a freelance artist or copywriter, you will probably work on a project-by-project basis for either an advertising agency or the advertiser. You will very likely do many of the same tasks that you would do if you were working for the client or agency.

Successful freelancing hinges on understanding and executing with speed whatever is needed. There is no employer to train you. If you want to freelance, you must know your business. Of course, unlike a steady job with an advertiser or agency, you will have to find the work yourself. You cannot wait until someone calls. The skill with which you make and expand your job contacts will be the deciding factor in how successful you are at freelancing.

Join a professional organization and keep track of former colleagues and friends who know your capabilities and understand your talent.

Freelancing or starting your own agency has many advantages. If you are good and develop a reputation with a following, you have the potential to earn more than an employee. Of course, unlike a steady job, you can't always count on a paycheck coming in once or twice a month. There are many peaks and valleys, and you need the financial resources and steady emotions to carry you through the low periods. Sometimes there will be no work and sometimes people will take a long time to pay, so you must have financial reserves to carry you through the slow times. You also have the satisfaction and flexibility of being your own boss. You may also find yourself working harder than ever. This will undoubtedly be true during the first years, when you are attempting to establish yourself. Since you will probably have to pay the media, suppliers, and operating expenses long before you have received payment from your clients, it is essential that you have enough cash reserves; at least six months of estimated operating expenses is a must to set up shop. Also, since it takes time to get clients and develop a reasonable flow of steady business and since some clients will take up to four or five months to pay their bills, you would be wise to have a resource to turn to if further capital is needed. Do not forget that you have to eat and pay your staff as well. So by all means, take the plunge if you have the experience and think the time is right. But before you jump, test the water.

Once an agency has been in business for a while, its owners may want to become members of the AAAA. Gaining membership in this organization is a good bit harder than getting started in the business. The agency must be able to demonstrate its financial stability, must be prepared to adhere to the AAAA code of practice, must be nominated by some other agency, must be approved by other members, and must be able to secure references from a number of media with which it has done business. In short, it must be recognized as responsible, established, and professional.

If you decide that starting your own agency would be a great idea, be sure that you consult a lawyer, get the support of a banker, and establish satisfactory credit. It is too important and risky a step to take without doing proper planning in advance. Still, it could be the most rewarding and satisfying step you ever take in the course of establishing your career in advertising.

OPPORTUNITIES IN SMALLER AGENCIES

Your first thought when beginning to look for a job in advertising will probably be, "How can I get a job at a large, big-city agency?" Before focusing your job search at the larger agencies, be sure to take a look at the unique opportunities at a smaller agency or even a small-town agency.

There are many agencies across the country that offer a different but no less challenging work environment than the larger agencies. These smaller agencies may be found in the major advertising cities or in smaller cities and towns across the country. The competition for jobs in this environment is just as fierce as the competition for jobs in a larger agency. What you will find in a smaller agency that you won't find in a larger agency is a less structured work environment and a broader spectrum of diversified work. With less staff, a small agency offers one the opportunity to learn and master many facets of the advertising business that you are unlikely to experience at a large agency. And remember, just because an agency is small does not mean that it lacks a top-notch staff with big-agency talent. Working at a small agency may mean a step down in size, but not necessarily in the quality of the work.

A good idea when looking for a job at a small agency is to take a look at the agency's client list. Find an agency that has a good variety of clients because a diversified pool of clients means a fuller working experience for you. Client lists can be found in *The Agency Red Book*, which you will find in most libraries and in most agencies. With larger agencies, the client list is usually wide and diversified. Just as there are advantages and disadvantages to working in a large firm, there are advantages and disadvantages in a smaller firm.

SALARIES

The economic recession that hit advertising agencies hard during 2001–02 had a chilling effect on industry salaries and employment. Some of the largest agencies reduced their employee head count and froze salaries for senior and mid-level executives. Many senior executives deferred their usual bonuses and profit sharing until 2003. As a result, the employees with six-figure salaries saw little or no growth in their income, and many employees in account services or media sales, where personal income is linked to their ability to deliver new business, saw their income drop dramatically.

Entry-level employees, however, were less affected than more experienced staff. Entry-level salaries have remained virtually unchanged since 2000, and many agencies continued to hire entry-level employees even as they were laying off older, more experienced employees as a way of reducing overall payroll costs.

Entry-level salaries range from $18,000 to $25,000 for new employees with minimal professional training, but marketing or advertising college graduates with a good portfolio started higher up the ladder at better salaries. Production employees and art assistants stayed near the bottom of the scale.

In 2003, however, agencies began to budget for increases, according to a survey conducted by *Advertising Age,* with an average raise of about 2 percent. However, agencies also linked more of its compensation to development of new business, so account services staff having greater contact with clients are likely to make more than others.

WRAP-UP

Okay, now you've had your introduction to the advertising business. The rest is up to you. If you are in the midst of finishing your education, then apply yourself and learn as much as possible. If you're in the job market now, either for an entry-level position or to further your career, plunge ahead and accept the challenge with enthusiasm. I wish you good luck! I am sure that you will find your career in advertising to be challenging, exciting, and rewarding.

ORGANIZATIONS FOR SPECIFIC GROUPS

The organizations cited here provide information on career planning, training, or public policy support for specific groups.

The Disabled
Office of Disability Employment Policy, 1331 F Street, NW, Third Floor, Washington, DC 20004.

This division of the U.S. Department of Labor is dedicated to expanding access to training, education, employment supports, assistive technology, integrated employment, entrepreneurial development, and small-business opportunities for the disabled.

The Blind

Information on the free national reference and referral service provided by the Federation of the Blind can be obtained by contacting Job Opportunities for the Blind (JOB), National Federation of the Blind, 1800 Johnson Street, Baltimore, MD 21230 (phone: toll-free 1-800-638-7518).

Minorities

The National Urban League is a nonprofit community-based social service and civil rights organization that assists African Americans in the achievement of social and economic equality. There are 113 local affiliates throughout the country that provide services related to employment and job training, education, and career development. Contact the affiliate nearest you for information or write to the National Association for the Advancement of Colored People (NAACP), 4805 Mount Hope Drive, Baltimore, MD 21215-3297.

Older Workers

National Association of Older Workers Employment Services, c/o National Council on the Aging, 409 3rd Street, SW, Suite 200, Washington, DC 20024.

For publications on job opportunities, contact the American Association of Retired Persons, Workforce Program Department, 601 E Street, NW, Floor A5, Washington, DC 20049.

Association Nacional por Personas Mayores (National Association for Hispanic Elderly), 2727 W. 6th Street, Suite 270, Los Angeles, CA 90057: this organization specifically serves low-income, minority persons who are fifty-five years of age and older.

National Caucus/Center on Black Aged, Inc., 1424 K Street, NW, Suite 500, Washington, DC 20005

Veterans

Contact the nearest regional office of the Department of Veterans Affairs.

APPENDIX

A

RECOMMENDED READING, WEBSITES, DIRECTORIES, AND PERIODICALS

RECOMMENDED READING

Field, Shelly. *Career Opportunities in Advertising and Public Relations*, 3rd ed. New York: Facts on File, 2002.

Haeglem, Katie. *E-Advertising and E-Marketing: Online Opportunities*. New York: Rosen Publication, 2001.

Lawrence, Mary Wells. *A Big Life in Advertising*. New York: Knopf, 2002.

Lederman, Eva. *Careers in Advertising*. New York: Princeton Review, 1998.

Neidle, Andrea. *How to Get into Advertising: A Guide to Careers in Advertising, Media and Marketing Communications*. Stamford, Conn. Thomson Learning, 2000.

Ogilvy, David. *Confessions of an Advertising Man*, 2nd ed. NTC, 1987.

_____. *Ogilvy on Advertising*. New York: Vintage Books, 1985.

O'Guin, Thomas. *Advertising and Integrated Brand Promotion*. Stamford, Conn.: Thomson, 2003.

Paetro, Maxine. *How to Put Your Book Together and Get a Job in Advertising*. Chicago: Copy Workshop, 2002.

Smith, Jeanette. *Breaking into Advertising: How to Market Yourself Like a Professional*. Lawrenceville, N.J.: Peterson's Guides, 1998.

The Wet Feet Insider's Guide to Careers in Advertising. San Francisco: Wet Feet, 2002.

White, Roderick. *Advertising: What It Is and How to Do It*. New York: McGraw-Hill, 1993.

WEBSITES

Advertising Council (adcouncil.org)
Advertising Research Council (arfsite.org)
Advertising Educational Foundation (aef.com)
American Advertising Federation (aaf.org)
Association for Interactive Marketing (interactivehq.org)
Association of Direct Marketing (adworks.org)
Association of National Advertisers (ana.net)
Wet Feet (wetfeet.com)

DIRECTORIES

Newspaper Rates and Data
    1700 Higgins Road
    DesPlaines, IL 60018

Standard Directory of Advertisers
    National Register Publishing Company
    121 Chanlon Road
    New Providence, NJ 07974

Standard Directory of Advertising Agencies
    National Register Publishing Company
    121 Chanlon Road
    New Providence, NJ 07974

Standard Rate and Data Service
    1700 Higgins Road
    DesPlaines, IL 60018

Working Press of the Nation
    Reed Reference Publishing
    121 Chanlon Road
    New Providence, NJ 07974

PERIODICALS

Ad Business Report, New York

Advertising Age, Crain Communications, Chicago

Adweek, Adweek Inc., New York

American Demographics, Ithaca, NY

Brandweek, Adweek Inc., New York

B2B, Crain Communications, Chicago

Creativity, Crain Communications, Chicago

Folio, Cowles Media Group, Stamford, CT

Graphic Arts Product News, MacLean Hunter Publishing, Chicago

Inside Media, Cowles Media Group, Stamford, CT

Journal of Advertising Research, Advertising Research Foundation,
   New York

Journal of Marketing, American Marketing Association, Chicago

Marketing and Media Decisions, Act III Publishing, New York

Marketing News, American Marketing Association, Chicago

PR Reporter, PR Publications Co., Exeter, NH

Public Relations Journal, Public Relations Society of America, New York

Quarterly Report: Association of National Advertisers, Advertising/
   Communications Times, Philadelphia

Sales and Marketing Management, Bill Communications, New York

A P P E N D I X

COLLEGE ADVERTISING PROGRAMS

A selected list of colleges offering programs in advertising is presented here. Every effort has been made to make this a comprehensive list, but as changes can occur rapidly, you should also check with local and state schools and with the American Advertising Federation for any additional choices at the time you wish to choose a school. Moreover, in addition to colleges offering advertising programs, many other schools have courses in marketing, journalism, design, and other advertising-related subjects, which you will also want to investigate.

Alabama

University of Alabama
    Tuscaloosa, AL 35486
    www.ua.edu

Arizona

Northern Arizona University
    Flagstaff, AZ 86001
    www.nau.edu

Arkansas

University of Arkansas/Little Rock
    Little Rock, AR 72204
    www.ualr.edu

California

Chapman University
Orange, CA 92666
www.chapman.edu

Pepperdine University
Malibu, CA 90265
www.pepperdine.edu

San Jose State University
San Jose, CA 95192
www.sjsu.edu

University of San Francisco
San Francisco, CA 94117
www.usfca.edu

Colorado

University of Colorado
Boulder, CO 80309
www.colorado.edu

Connecticut

University of Bridgeport
Bridgeport, CT 06602
www.bridgeport.edu

Florida

University of Florida
Gainesville, FL 32611
www.ufl.edu

Georgia

University of Georgia
Athens, GA 30602
www.uga.edu

Illinois

Bradley University
  Peoria, IL 61625
  www.bradley.edu

Columbia College Chicago
  Chicago, IL 60605
  www.colum.edu

Northwestern University
  Evanston, IL 60201
  www.northwestern.edu

Southern Illinois University
  Carbondale, IL 62901
  www.siu.edu

University of Illinois
  Urbana, IL 61801
  www.uiuc.edu/index.html

Indiana

Ball State University
  Muncie, IN 47306
  www.bsu.edu

Purdue University
  West Lafayette, IN 47907
  www.purdue.edu

Iowa

Drake University
  Des Moines, IA 50311
  www.drake.edu

Kentucky

Murray State University
  Murray, KY 42071
  www.murraystate.edu

University of Kentucky
  Lexington, KY 40506
  www.uky.edu

Western Kentucky University
  Bowling Green, KY 42101
  www.wku.edu

Louisiana

Louisiana State University
  Baton Rouge, LA 70803
  www.lsu.edu

Maryland

University of Baltimore
  Baltimore, MD 21228
  www.ubalt.edu

Massachusetts

Boston University
  Boston, MA 02215
  www.bu.edu

Simmons College
  Boston, MA 02115
  www.simmons.edu

Michigan

Ferris State College
  Big Rapids, MI 49307
  www.ferris.edu

Michigan State University
  East Lansing, MI 48824
  www.msu.edu/home

Western Michigan University
  Kalamazoo, MI 49001
  www.wmich.edu

Minnesota

University of Minnesota
Minneapolis, MN 55455
www.umn.edu

University of St. Thomas
St. Paul, MN 55105
www.stthomas.edu

Winona State University
Winona, MN 55987
www.winona.msus.edu

Mississippi

University of Southern Mississippi
Hattiesburg, MS 39401
www.usm.edu

Nebraska

University of Nebraska
Lincoln, NE 68588
www.unl.edu/unlpub/index.shtml

New Hampshire

Franklin Pierce College
Rindge, NH 03461
www.fpc.edu

New Jersey

Thomas Edison State College
Trenton, NJ 08608
www.tesc.edu

New York

College of New Rochelle
New Rochelle, NY 10801
www.cnr.edu

New York Institute of Technology
   Old Westbury, NY 11568
   www.nyit.edu

Syracuse University
   Syracuse, NY 13210
   www.syr.edu

North Carolina

Campbell University
   Buies Creek, NC 27506
   www.campbell.edu

North Dakota

University of North Dakota
   Grand Forks, ND 58202
   www.und.edu

Ohio

Columbus College of Art and Design
   Columbus, OH 43215
   www.ccad.edu

Kent State University
   Kent, OH 44242
   www.kent.edu

Marietta College
   Marietta, OH 45750
   www.marietta.edu

Ohio University
   Athens, OH 47501
   www.ohiou.edu

Youngstown State University
   Youngstown, OH 44555
   www.ysu.edu

Oklahoma

University of Oklahoma
Norman, OK 73019
www.ou.edu

Pennsylvania

Cedar Crest College
Allentown, PA 18104
www.cedarcrest.edu

Marywood University
Scranton, PA 18509
www.marywood.edu

Pennsylvania State University
University Park, PA 16802
www.psu.edu

South Carolina

University of South Carolina
Columbia, SC 29208
www.sc.edu

South Dakota

South Dakota State University
Brookings, SD 57007
www3.sdstate.edu

Tennessee

Middle Tennessee State University
Murfreesboro, TN 37132
www.mtsu.edu

University of Tennessee
Knoxville, TN 37919
www.utk.edu

Texas

Abilene Christian University
Abilene, TX 79699
www.acu.edu

Southern Methodist University
Dallas, TX 75275
www.smu.edu

Texas Tech University
Lubbock, TX 79409
www.ttu.edu

University of Texas at Austin
Austin, TX 78712
www.utexas.edu

Utah

Weber State University
Ogden, UT 84408
www.weber.edu

Virginia

Liberty University
Lynchberg, VA 24506
www.liberty.edu

Wisconsin

Marquette University
Milwaukee, WI 53233
www.marquette.edu

APPENDIX

C

NATIONAL GROUPS AND ASSOCIATIONS

The Advertising Council
261 Madison Avenue, 11th Floor
New York, NY 10016
www.adcouncil.org

Advertising Research Foundation
641 Lexington Avenue
New York, NY 10022
www.arfsite.org

American Advertising Federation
1101 Vermont Avenue, NW, Suite 500
Washington, DC 20005-6306
www.aaf.org

American Association of Advertising Agencies
405 Lexington Avenue, 18th Floor
New York, NY 10174
www.aaaa.org

American Marketing Association
250 S. Wacker Drive, Suite 200
Chicago, IL 60606
www.marketingpower.com

Association of National Advertisers
    708 Third Avenue
    New York, NY 10017
    www.ana.net

Council of Sales Promotion Agencies
    750 Summer Street
    Stamford, CT 06901

Direct Marketing Association
    1120 Avenue of the Americas
    New York, NY 10036
    www.the-dma.org

International Advertising Association
    521 Fifth Avenue, Suite 1807
    New York, NY 10175
    www.iaaglobal.org

Magazine Publishers of America
    919 Third Avenue
    New York, NY 10022
    www.magazine.org

National Association of Broadcasters
    1771 N Street, NW
    Washington, DC 20036
    www.nab.org

National Association of Publisher Representatives
    320 E. 42nd Street, Suite 402
    New York, NY 10017
    www.naprassoc.com

National Cable & Telecommunications Association
    1724 Massachusetts Avenue, NW
    Washington, DC 20036
    www.ncta.com

Outdoor Advertising Association of America
1850 M. Street, NW, Suite 1040
Washington, DC 20036
www.oaaa.org

Point-of-Purchase Advertising Institute
1660 L Street, NW
Washington, DC. 20036
www.popai.com

Promotion Marketing Association of America
322 8th Avenue, Suite 1201
New York, NY 10001
www.pmalink.org

Public Relations Society of America
33 Irving Place
New York, NY 10003
www.prsa.org

Radio Advertising Bureau
1300 Greenway Drive, Suite 500
Irving, TX 75038
www.rab.com

Retail Advertising Association
333 N. Michigan Avenue, Suite 3000
Chicago, IL 60601
www.rama-nrf.org

Television Bureau of Advertising
3 East 54th Street
New York, NY 10022
www.tvb.or

ABOUT THE AUTHOR

S. William "Bill" Pattis enjoys telling the story of how he started his lifetime career in publishing and advertising. At the age of eight, he sold the *Saturday Evening Post* for a nickel a copy to commuters at the neighborhood train station in Chicago's Hyde Park community. At twelve, he was a co-owner of a corner newsstand.

His career came to a standstill for the next nine years as he finished high school, served in Europe as a combat engineer during World War II, and obtained a degree in marketing and management at the University of Illinois. While in college, he immersed himself in extracurricular activities that contributed much to his flair for advertising and promotion.

His first postcollege job was in Chicago selling advertising for United Business Publications at $40 a week. In the evenings, he continued his studies in graduate school at Northwestern University. Progressing rapidly, at age twenty-nine he was moved to New York by his employer to become publisher of *Photographic Trade News*. In quick succession, his responsibilities were expanded to assume the full publishing responsibility for five magazines.

At age thirty-three, he returned to Chicago to establish The Pattis Group, which he headed as chairman and chief executive officer. Under his direction, the firm became the world's largest in magazine advertising sales, with offices in Chicago, New York, Los Angeles, Atlanta, Miami, Honolulu, Toronto, London, and Paris. The firm was sold and became known as 3M/Pattis and functioned as an operating division of the Advertising Services Group of the giant 3M Company. As a result of this work, the author was involved on a daily basis with most national advertisers and probably all of the advertising agencies in America. The scope of these activities has formed the basis for much of the knowledge and information found in this book.

The author's writings include many articles appearing in the advertising press and four other books on advertising and media. His speaking engagements have included appearances before the National Association of Publishers Representatives, the Overseas Press and Media Association, and the International Media Buyers' Association. He participated in the first Face-to-Face International conference in The Hague, Netherlands, and has been a principal speaker at the annual meeting of the Periodical Publishers Association of the United Kingdom. In 1988, he participated in the first U.S.-U.S.S.R. bilateral talks in Moscow involving members of American print media and their Soviet counterparts. In 1991, he served as chairman of the U.S. delegation for follow-up talks in both Moscow and Washington, D.C.

As is typical for many people in communications, he has served on various civic and charitable committees throughout his business life. In the late 1960s and early 1970s, he received commendations from Vice President Hubert Humphrey and Vice President Spiro Agnew for his work on the President's Council for Youth Opportunity. For six years, he was chairman of the Book and Library Committee of the United States Information Agency, and he served on the Executive Committee of the Publishing Hall of Fame. In 1991, he received a presidential appointment from former President George H. W. Bush to serve on the National Security Education Board.

His other business interests have included being president of P-B Communications, publisher of Chicago's *North Shore* magazine, and having founded and been president of NTC Publishing Group, former publisher of VGM Career Books.

His current activities include being vice chairman of Professional Media Group of Norwalk, Connecticut, and active service on the Board of Trustees in Rancho Mirage, California.